Making a Leap –
Theatre of Empowerment

of related interest

Trust and Power
Taking Care of Ourselves Through Drama
Penny Casdagli
ISBN 1 85302 556 9 pb

Arts Approaches to Conflict
Edited by Marian Liebmann
ISBN 1 85302 293 4 pb

Group Work with Children and Adolescents
A Handbook
Edited by Kedar Nath Dwivedi
ISBN 1 85302 157 1 pb

Violence in Children and Adolescents
Edited by Ved Varma
ISBN 1 85302 344 2 pb

Troubles of Children and Adolescents
Edited by Ved Varma
ISBN 1 85302 323 X pb

Making a Leap – Theatre of Empowerment

A Practical Handbook for Drama and Theatre Work with Young People

Sara Clifford and Anna Herrmann

Foreword by Alec Davison

Jessica Kingsley Publishers
London and Philadelphia

First published in the United Kingdom in 1999 by
Jessica Kingsley Publishers Ltd
116 Pentonville Road
London N1 9JB, England
and
325 Chestnut Street,
Philadelphia, PA 19106, USA.

www.jkp.com

Copyright © 1999 Leap Theatre Workshop

Library of Congress Cataloging in Publication Data
A CIP catalogue record for this book is available from the Library of Congress

British Library Cataloguing in Publication Data
Herrmann, Anna
Making a leap: theatre of empowerment: a practical handbook for creative drama work with young people
1.Theatre and youth – Handbooks, manuals, etc. 2.Drama in education – Handbooks, manuals, etc. 3.Psychodrama – Handbooks, manuals, etc.
I.Title II.Clifford Sara
792'.083

ISBN 1 85302 632 8

Printed and Bound in Great Britain by
Athenaeum Press, Gateshead, Tyne and Wear

CONTENTS

List of Figures   8

Preface   9

Foreword *Alec Davison*   11

The Leap Metaphor   13

INTRODUCTION

Background to Leap Theatre Workshop   15

Why Drama?   16

Devising Theatre   16

Theatre of Empowerment   17

The Participants   18

This Book and How to Use It   19

THE FACILITATOR'S GUIDE

Teacher or Director?   21

Why Facilitate?   21

The Lone Facilitator   22

Co-Facilitation   22

Boundaries   23

Golden Rules   23

Mistakes Procedure   25

Scapegoating   25

How to Structure a Workshop   26

Example Workshops   27

UNIT ONE: PREPARATION

Unit Guide   33

Introduction   33

Ready: Recruitment   33

Steady: The Introductory Workshop   37
Go: Creating a Safe Space   39
Games   40
Groundrules   62
Group Work   66
Closings   74
Action Research   79

UNIT TWO: TRAINING

Unit Guide   83
Introduction   83
Exploring the Theme   83
Physical and Vocal Warm-Ups   85
Theatre and Drama Techniques   92
Engendering Leadership: Training in Workshop Skills   125

UNIT THREE: DEVISING THE SHOW

Unit Guide   133
Introduction   133
Devising a Theatre Piece   133
Aims of the Work   134
A Framework for Educational Theatre   135
Rehearsals   161
Presentation   169
The Workshop   170

UNIT FOUR: THE TOUR

Unit Guide   177
Introduction   177
The Show and Notes   178
Preparation for the Tour   184
Continued Training and Group Cohesion   185
The Speak Out   189

UNIT FIVE: EVALUATION

Unit Guide   197
Introduction   197
Purposes of Evaluation   198

Evaluation Methods   199
Other Forms of Evaluation   205
Example of Evaluation Form   205

UNIT SIX: CONFRONTING CONFLICT
Unit Guide   208
Introduction   209
What is Conflict?   210
Strategies for Addressing Conflict   212
Conflict Scenarios   222
Moving On From Conflict   225

UNIT SEVEN: ENDING
Unit Guide   231
Introduction   231
Guidance and Support   231
Recognising Achievements   234
Follow-Up   235

PRACTICALITIES
Contents   237
Introduction   237
Equal Opportunities Policy   237
Funding   238
The Budget   238
Booking a Tour   241
Health and Safety/First Aid   241
Insurance   241
Space   242
Costume and Set   242
Tour Transport   243
Supervision   243
Documentation   243
Venue Evaluation   245
Tidying Up   246

EPILOGUE

Summing Up   249
Resources   249
Organisations   250
List of Games and Exercises   253

List of Figures

1.1	Distributing flyers	35
1.2	'Can I interest you in a project?'	36
1.3	Grandma listens out	36
1.4	Points of contact	44
1.5	Participants create their own group agreement	64
1.6	Brainstorming	67
1.7	Sharing personal stories	73
2.1	A drumming workshop	108
2.2	A media machine	111
2.3	Sculpting	124
3.1	Three vital elements of theatre	136
3.2	Character work	145
3.3	Voices in the head technique	151
3.4	The 'Dole Boys' run the benefit office	155
3.5	A group scene	158
3.6	The backdrop	170
4.1	Unloading the van	179
4.2	Introducing the show	182
4.3	Running a workshop	184
4.4	Additional training	189
4.5	The Speak Out	192
5.1	The best moment of the project	201
6.1	Attack and avoid	214
7.1	Thinking about the next step	233
8.1	Booking a tour	239

Preface

Making a Leap is aimed primarily at drama workers, youth work professionals, teachers, theatre practitioners and volunteers – in fact anyone who wishes to use drama and theatre in their work with young people.

The book was conceived as the culmination of the 'Acting on Homelessness' project, a five-year plan of work undertaken by Leap Theatre Workshop, using drama and theatre to explore youth homelessness with groups of young unemployed and homeless people. Each training project looked at some of the different experiences of young people affected by homelessness, including young women, black people, drug users and people leaving care and prison, and devised a peer education theatre piece to tour homeless hostels, schools and youth clubs with an accompanying workshop.

Over the course of the five years, we formulated a model for training young people in theatre and drama skills and workshop facilitation skills, through synthesising techniques drawn from the strong history of theatre-in-education in this country with the work we developed ourselves, and we appreciatively acknowledge the ideas originally conceived by others. We created a structure for a training project that we felt would be helpful for anyone wanting to do this kind of work with young people, a step-by-step process that would serve as a practical guide embodying good practice, both for experienced practitioners and those starting out, and which could be used with different groups and adapted to different length projects.

We have made our approach holistic, offering not just drama skills, but linking this training to personal development, group work, conflict resolution and facilitation skills, to create a broader experience that we liken to making a leap, a jump to a different place. It is this process that we call Theatre of Empowerment – a personal, social and political empowerment – that is, ultimately, a tool for social change: a proactive, potentially life-changing experience, that truly empowers the participants to recognise that they have choices in life and to consider these choices from a new perspective.

We aimed to make this book an accessible and practical handbook to this process, and we hope that readers will find it a useful resource in their work.

We would like to acknowledge Alec Davison, the founder of Leap Theatre Workshop (and the Leaveners) and guiding light behind the work; Augusto

Boal, for his inspirational work around the world; Nic Fine and Fiona Macbeth, for the work they developed previously for Leap; all the staff, trainers and Committee members at Leap, especially Helen Carmichael, Tina Helfrich and Pete Lawson; the directors of the earlier Leap projects, for the work they undertook which we were able to build on; and, above all, all the young people who have taken part in projects over the years – thank you!

We would also like to thank the funders who made the 'Acting on Homelessness' project possible and so contributed greatly to the development of these materials. These include specifically: The Calouste Gulbenkian Foundation, The Carnegie UK Trust, Quaker Homeless Action, The Princes Trust, William A. Cadbury Charitable Trust and The Lansbury House Trust Fund.

The illustrations for the book were drawn by Dee Shulman. The photographs were taken by Frank Herrmann.

Sara Clifford and Anna Herrmann
London, 1997

Foreword

The only certainty about the future is its uncertainty. Yet it seems safe to predict that no brake can be applied to the accelerating rate of social change. Humanity's infinite capacity for curiosity and ingenuity will ensure that new knowledge and technological inventiveness continue to flood the world. The earth's resources decline, populations explode and paid full-time employment for all is a golden dream. Whether many of our young people swim or flounder as the microchip, robotisation and globalised multinationals determine everyone's lifestyle will depend on our foresight and humanity today.

Improvisation, imagination and working together are human skills that we shall all need in abundance. They are also the skills that lie at the heart of creative drama and community theatre. This is unsurprising as those educational forms are nothing but a distillation of humanity's innate and evolutionary spur to play and shape and share. But in an educational system which is increasingly instrumental, individualistic and competitive in its narrow vocational thrust rather than being holistic and cooperative, nourishing both inner and outer human needs, the Theatre of Empowerment has yet to be honoured with a central place. This book is a prophetic and practical plea asking why this should be so.

For all the many tools in the hands of those involved in social change, whether educators or community workers of all kinds, whether professional or volunteers, whether young or old, one of the most vital and powerful is that of group play-making and performance. 'Barefoot' theatre troupes world-wide entertain and provoke, raising consciousness within the group and within the community. They find their voice about their lives and speak that new-found truth to power. But they also find each other, forge friendships, celebrate and taste of transformation: they come to know empowerment.

The means to do so, the processes that are used, come from tradition and intuition but increasingly also from the international network and grapevine. In Britain everyone in the field will acknowledge Peter Slade, Brian Way, Dorothy Heathcote, Gavin Bolton and the theatre-in-education pioneers of the 1960s and 1970s. But the late 1980s and 1990s saw cuts upon cuts and in order to survive educational drama had to embrace the academic. So the dynamic shifted back again to theatre practitioners such as Augusto Boal in

Brazil, Jacques Lecoq in Paris and at home a handful of experimental independent groups, devising new forms of 'poor' theatre, often while working with the unemployed, such as Leap Theatre Workshop, founded in 1987.

Leap magpies from the past, as each new company must, but it equally values process and product, drama and theatre, affirmation and aesthetics. Over ten years of nitty-gritty work at the coalface of young people's disadvantage and exclusion it has found its own idiosyncratic voice. Its authenticity comes from addressing contemporary hot issues with those caught up in them. It explores alternatives to violence and confronting conflict creatively. It has much that is important to say to all new training and volunteering projects, whether Welfare-to-Work and its successors, Citizens Service, the Princes' or Community Service Volunteers, and penal projects of every kind, as well as to secondary, further or higher education and the youth service at large. No vision of the future can ignore the crucial role of volunteering. A ten-week 'Making a Leap' project is the richest possible form of personal and social education while giving service to the community.

From this original London Leap company may a host of nation-wide and international Leap companies spring. Such a grassroot network of new possibilities is bound to contribute to the betterment of our communities as they are forced to develop creative human strategies to face the future. That is our leap of faith.

Alec Davison
Founder of Leap

The Leap Metaphor

THE FIRST STEPS

The first steps towards *the leap* are making the decision to move forward and finding the courage to leave behind our existing way of life. We must then make preparations, so that *the leap* can take place on solid ground.

TRAINING TO MAKE THE LEAP

Once the groundwork has been done and the first steps taken, we can continue to prepare ourselves properly for making *the leap*. Now we must train mentally, physically and spiritually to make ourselves strong and ready to confront the change that lies ahead.

THE RUN-UP

After we have prepared ourselves through training, we can start making the run-up to *the leap*. Now we have the skills and the confidence to take firm steps in the right direction and build the necessary momentum.

THE LEAP

During *the leap* itself, we are suspended in mid air, feeling nervous and exhilarated, yet with energy and power in our flight. We are in the midst of the experience, not sure of what the impact of *the leap* will be on ourselves or on the people around us, but knowing that the inevitable movement of *the leap* will propel us forward to our landing.

THE LANDING

At the end of *the leap*, we land in a new place, a different place to where we jumped from. Now we have the chance to look back to where we have come from, see the distance we've come and congratulate ourselves on our achievements.

STUMBLING

Things might not be as smooth as you hope either during the run-up or *the leap* itself. You might stumble, fall and hurt yourself and need support and help in getting back on your feet. Try to take the opportunity for learning what lies in the fall, rather than becoming stuck in the hurt and pain.

THE NEXT STEP

Now we can look around at the new landscape we have arrived in, and decide what our choices are. This will help us to begin preparing to make the next leap.

Introduction

Making a leap symbolises a jumping off into the unknown. It is the creative process of change which has the power to transform our lives, enabling us to see the world from a different perspective and so empowering us to make new choices.

We can *leap for joy*, or *leap in the dark* but we are advised to *look before we leap*. It is the spirit of these expressions that is contained within a Leap project. When we look before we leap, we prepare ourselves for the event, making sure we are ready and that the leap will prove a success. Having a clear vision of the path ahead enables us to feel confident about where we are heading. A leap for joy suggests celebration; we are exuberant, in the air, powerful and filled with energy. We also have a clarity of vision as we are high up and no longer crowded by obstacles in our view. Taking a leap in the dark, however, is a risk: we do not know where we will land or what we will find there. It is an uncertain leap – exciting, challenging. When we land we may have a new outlook and see things in a different light. With every leap there is a risk as well as an opportunity. We must embrace what frightens us as well as what excites us. It is only then that we will be able to grow, learn, change and prepare to make the next leap.

BACKGROUND TO LEAP THEATRE WORKSHOP

Leap Theatre Workshop was established in 1987, by the Leaveners (a Quaker Community Arts Charity), to explore the causes of and alternatives to violence and conflict through drama and theatre. Drawing on the fields of drama education, youth work and the peace movement, Leap aims to provide young people, of 14–25 years, with accessible, empowering and relevant training and volunteering opportunities in community arts, where their needs and ideas can be realised and their voices heard. The young people volunteer to participate in the project, making the choice and the commitment to be there. This volunteering ethos is crucial to the good practice of the work.

Over the years, Leap has worked in care units, schools, youth clubs, homeless hostels and prisons, with young offenders, young unemployed people and young refugees. We tour performances and workshops nationally; we run courses and conferences for young people and those who work with them; and we host 'Speak Out' events for young people to voice their opinions to local MPs, councillors, the media and youth/social workers. The body of the ideas in this book were developed during the 'Acting on Homelessness' project (1993–1997) which worked with young unemployed and homeless people through theatre and drama for empowerment to raise awareness of youth homelessness and influence decision making.

The underlying fundamental belief which feeds Leap's work is that everyone has creative potential and it is the realisation of this potential that benefits the individual, the community and society at large.

WHY DRAMA?

Drama engages both the head and the heart. Learning through drama relies on the active involvement of our mind, body, feelings and spirit. In the realm of imagined experience, we take on roles of other characters and experience different situations, so that our understanding of ourselves, of others and of the world we live in grows. Drama provides an opportunity to address moral dilemmas, to express our feelings, to be creative and to explore new ideas and ways of being. Drama demands interaction between people – it is a social process – and for this reason is ideally suited to working with a group.

And, of course, drama is fun!

DEVISING THEATRE

When devising theatre at Leap, the group make a creative statement on an issue which is important to them. There is no writer, the group are not given a script and they are not given parts. These elements, which are aspects of mainstream theatre, are subverted here by drawing on the traditions of theatre-in-education and the alternative theatre of the 1970s, developing the script as the group discuss, improvise and rehearse what they want to say. The characters are created as group members research the theme and draw on their own lives, reflecting their experiences in the stories they choose to tell. It is an ensemble piece, and everyone has a role to play – they are all 'stars'. Devising theatre allows the young people to be in control of the product they create, supported and directed by the facilitators. There is a strong sense of participation, ownership and empowerment.

THEATRE OF EMPOWERMENT

Theatre of Empowerment develops young people's personal, social and political being. Through bringing our mind, body and spirit to the drama, we gain insight into ourselves (personal). Through working with others to create a play within the discipline of theatre, we develop skills to relate to people and build relationships based on trust, support, honesty and understanding (social). Finally, as we take our performance out to the wider community, we make ourselves heard in the public arena, allowing others to engage with our views and concerns and impacting on the world we live in (political). It is the ability of theatre to transform the inner self, the group and society at large that makes it so powerful and appropriate a medium for work with young people.

The process is as fundamental as the product created, but the dynamic between the two is always a challenge for the facilitator and for the young people. The process alone, without the focus of the theatre piece to motivate the group, risks becoming therapy. The theatre piece alone without the group's experience of the process will lack vision and ownership. It is the balancing of the two that ensures neither suffers.

Theatre of Empowerment encourages young people to believe in themselves, developing self-esteem and self-confidence. This enables group members to value their own and others' contributions, learning to respect who they are and what they bring. It is not about 'egos', it is about participation, expression and communication. Initially the group members communicate with each other, listening, speaking about their feelings and thoughts and sharing their experiences creatively. The performance/workshop is their chance to communicate with the outside world, enabling dialogue and exchange to take place. The quality of the play needs to be of a high standard to ensure that their voice comes across with clarity and vision. Theatre offers the group a platform, an audience and a chance to be heard. Group members experience the power implicit in educating and creating a positive learning opportunity for others, through voicing their own experiences on stage. By gaining a sense of their own power and self-worth, they are able to see the control they can have over their own lives and to recognise the choices that are available to them and the past choices that they have made; for some young people this may be the first time they have experienced this.

Theatre of Empowerment is about building a community, where each member has equal rights and responsibilities, and a spirit of cooperation and support is aspired to. Decisions are made as a group, either by consensus (agreement through discussion and dialogue) or by majority vote, and the ownership of these decisions, actions and statements lies with the group.

Participation from every individual in the group is fundamental to the process – and ultimately the success of the theatre piece relies on this group effort and mutual need. The community is one of diversity, where different backgrounds, needs, cultures and abilities are accepted and welcomed. It is an inclusive community which aims to counteract the experiences of isolation and exclusion that result from living in our society.

The community needs to be a space which is safe enough for people to be challenged and to take real risks. A safe space is created when we believe that our actions are not being judged and that our opinions are respected, despite their difference; when we feel physically safe and can trust those around us. If someone laughs at something we said, or lets us down by breaking a confidence, then we may no longer feel safe enough to share other experiences.

Theatre of Empowerment doesn't work with a grandiose set, elaborate costumes or within a theatre venue, resulting in the ultimate 'poor' theatre. This derives from the Polish theatre director Grotowski, whose experimental work reacted against the 'wealth' of the contemporary theatre and envisioned a 'poor' theatre which relies solely on the body and mind of the actor in a bare space, whether it be a hostel, a classroom or a youth club. This demonstrates to both actors and audience that theatre can be created by anyone and needs only the actor and the open space. It also acts as a metaphor for politics, for it is a democracy which functions on a local level, despite, or maybe because of, its poverty. It's not up to anyone else – it is up to you!

This book is the practical embodiment of these philosophies. It aims to provide the facilitator with a process of working which holds empowerment as its key.

THE PARTICIPANTS

The exercises in this manual assume a certain level of mobility among participants, but many exercises are adaptable for use with wheelchair users or by those with visual or hearing impairments. These adjustments have not been detailed and you, as the facilitator, will need to adapt the exercises to your group, as appropriate, assuming the space is accessible.

Leap projects bring together groups of young people from different backgrounds and a range of experiences, including young people at risk of homelessness, drug use, offending behaviour, and/or unemployment. This is one of its greatest strengths in that people bring different qualities and learn to work together with others, perhaps outside their normal peer group. However, it can also cause problems as participants work at different speeds, have different levels of ability, skills and experience and have different support needs. Some participants may also bring mental health problems and it is important, where possible, to ascertain the area of need in advance, so you can offer support accordingly. This may mean being in contact with someone's key worker, social worker or probation officer – with the permission of, and in consultation with, the individual concerned – as well as having information available on relevant agencies to refer participants to, if necessary (*see also* Practicalities).

THIS BOOK AND HOW TO USE IT

This book offers the reader a comprehensive way of devising issue-based theatre with young people. The model is based on a ten-week full-time Leap project which involves three weeks of group work and training, three weeks of devising and rehearsing, and four weeks of touring. Within this, we work with the group for four days a week and use the fifth day for the facilitator's planning and reflection. This time-scale has proved the most effective. You may be devising a theatre piece with your group for one day, a weekend, a week or a number of sessions over a certain period. In any of these situations, it is preferable to follow through the leap analogy, drawing on aspects of each unit to include groundwork, preparation, training and follow-up.

However, it is possible to approach the material in a very different way and to apply it to your individual circumstances. You may choose to use the manual as a toolbox and select individual exercises to use. This is appropriate for one-off workshop sessions or work that is not geared towards devising a piece.

Each unit offers an introduction and a detailed outline of the work undertaken. The exercises are presented under the following headings:

Time:	this is the estimated time you need to allocate for the exercise, excluding the suggested development period.
Materials:	what you need to bring/provide.
Number in Group:	we have suggested a minimum number of group members for each exercise and assumed a maximum number of 20.
Aim:	this is a short description of the exercise and what its purpose is.
Directions:	how to run the exercise.
Variations:	other approaches to the exercise.

Feedback and Discussion: where appropriate we have suggested possible feedback questions to encourage reflection.

Development: suggestions for further work.

Notes: practical issues that may arise or that you may wish to address in advance.

The Facilitator's Guide

TEACHER OR DIRECTOR?

The traditional teacher and director roles tend to be hierarchical ones, partly due to the demands of the settings where the work takes place, and partly because both are seen as high status leadership roles.

In this book, we have used the term 'facilitator' to indicate the person(s) organising and leading the work being undertaken. This role moves between those of director and teacher – at times you will be training the participants, giving information, teaching and polishing skills; and later on, as you rehearse the piece, you will also act as a director, offering a crucial outside eye in shaping the piece of theatre.

During the project you will draw on aspects of both roles, whilst moving towards a group ownership of, and responsibility for, the work, using the democratic process as a framework. Even traditional teacher/director concerns, such as time keeping, can be opened up to the group through the setting of groundrules, therefore reducing the level of the high status leadership.

You will be facilitating this process, as the group participants move towards the grander goals of personal, social and ultimately political empowerment – democracy in action!

Part of your job will be the practical one of translating the ideals outlined above into a real process: creating a space where the participants feel that their voices will be heard – a non-judgemental space, where their opinion is valued, perhaps for the first time, and where their experiences will inform the work being undertaken, enabling them to take an active role in their own development.

WHY FACILITATE?

It might be worth asking yourself why you want to facilitate a session or project. What is your agenda as leader of this group? What do you want to address and how? How have *you* reached this point in your life? What other areas of your life are informed by this agenda? Now try to assess what the group expects from you and the project, and then compare this with what you think the project is for and about. Obviously if they are very different, you need to think about ways of reconciling them. How will you address this?

THE LONE FACILITATOR

Facilitating a group by yourself has advantages and disadvantages. The advantages are that you can plan and adapt what you are doing according to the group – if only two people turn up that week, you can change your plans without consultation. Similarly, if a piece of work takes off in an unexpected but fascinating new direction, you can follow that direction and deepen the group's response to the work, again without explanation.

However, the disadvantages include the sheer pressure of taking all the responsibility all the time, which can feel very lonely and stressful.

If you are working by yourself, you need to find ways to support yourself: you will need to think about all the difficulties you are likely to encounter, such as problems within the workplace, or personal difficulties, such as controlling anger. Why not think about the word 'support', and brainstorm it for yourself – what does it mean to you? How can you support yourself when faced with difficulties? Later on in the project, set aside time to assess how you have supported yourself so far, and whether it needs changing.

It is really useful to ask someone you trust to act as an external supervisor. Perhaps you could meet with them once a week, and talk through the work, evaluating 'smiles and frowns', and assessing different ways forward.

It is also important to give yourself relaxation time, taking measures to relieve stress, both daily and weekly. How can you treat yourself at the end of a long hard week? It'll be worth it!

CO-FACILITATION

Working with a co-facilitator has some very obvious advantages – you can share the responsibility for the work, share the planning, share the actual leading of the sessions, and have someone to bounce ideas off, cry and laugh with at the end of the day! We are all trained to work individually, with the emphasis on our individual control and achievements. Co-facilitation is non-hierarchical, and empowering – you can learn from each other, support each other, and bring twice the experience and skills to the work. It also offers the opportunity to work with two groups separately, which then come back together, which is especially useful with large groups.

Obviously it is not easy the first time you work with someone, as you may be coming from different backgrounds and experiences. If possible, use some of your planning time to try some of the listening and trust exercises, sharing where you have come from, what your aims and objectives for the work are. Why have you chosen to work on this project? How do your agendas differ? How can you reconcile them? What are your favourite areas of work? What are your favourite methods?

It is important to be clear right from the start – if there is something you are unhappy or angry about, state it and address it. Use some of the exercises from the Conflict section, Unit Six, for a structure to support you. Don't sit on any differences or resentments, as they will affect your relationship and your work, and the group will probably notice, causing unsettled feelings and divisions. Include weekly and daily feedback sessions in your work, that can be used as mutual supervision sessions. However, it is also a good idea to have some form of external supervision in a structured environment – conflicts can be aired and addressed, and an outside eye cast on any difficulties with the group or the work.

Two personalities that complement each other and work together well offer the group a broader focus, and it is good to have a balance, such as male and female, black and white, though not essential. This teamwork can act as a non-hierarchical model of cooperation and lay the foundations for a long-term working relationship.

BOUNDARIES

Be sure to maintain clear boundaries between yourself as facilitator and the group. This means being clear about leisure time, for example spending breaks separately from the group: it is important to avoid confusion of roles and to allow the group the space to discuss the project informally. Also, be careful that group members do not see you as a counsellor with the expectations that accompany this role. The confidentiality and ongoing commitment that this role necessitates may conflict with your role as facilitator. You can refer people to more appropriate agencies if necessary.

GOLDEN RULES

Certain 'rules' will assist you in your work, such as:

- Give clear instructions for an exercise.
- Use appropriate language for your group.
- Never assume that everyone has understood – always check and repeat the instructions if necessary, perhaps using a different way of describing it.

- Use examples or demonstrations to make your instructions clear.

- Affirm individuals' and the group's work, offering suggestions and constructive criticism. Be specific and honest in your affirmation, for example, 'you remained very focused in that exercise', rather than a more general 'that was excellent!'

- Plan your session and set definite time limits on exercises and discussion time, allowing about 20 per cent extra contingency time. This will provide a strong framework.

- Sometimes exercises will run over the time allotted; negotiate with the group if extra time is needed.

- Equally, don't keep pushing an exercise to the allotted time, if it has obviously finished. Flexibility is the key. As you become more experienced, you will become more aware of the best time to finish an exercise, and better at finding the point when people have deepened their response, but not become bored by it.

- Allow adequate time for reflection and evaluation at the end of exercises, recognising that the learning process is not complete without this, and, particularly with devising, allow extra time for people with little experience of drama or working cooperatively.

- Find ways of communicating with your co-worker during a session.

- Ask open-ended questions that deepen responses and open up areas not previously thought of, for example, 'how did that feel?' rather than 'did you feel angry?' Try asking the same question in a different way.

- Always tell the group in advance of a small group/pairs exercise if you are going to ask them to feedback personal information to the whole group, so that they can decide what information to volunteer.

- Ensure that when people work in smaller groups and pairs they move around and work with different people to avoid cliques developing.

- When the group are working in small groups, go round and check on their progress.

- Keep in mind the aims of the exercise all the time, and keep people on track, while being flexible to their responses.

MISTAKES PROCEDURE

Acknowledging mistakes and taking responsibility for them is also empowering, both for the participants and yourself as facilitator (*see also* Groundrules, Unit One). Identify what was circumstantial and what was not, and think about what came from within the group, and what came from you. There is a useful structure for dealing with mistakes, where you don't make excuses, but take responsibility for what has happened and take steps to ensure the mistake is not made again:

- acknowledge what you have done
- accept responsibility for it
- clean up any mess you have made (have the necessary conversations etc.)
- see what you can do to make sure it will not happen again.

The group can learn from your lead to take responsibility for their mistakes.

SCAPEGOATING

Often a group, in the process of taking responsibility for itself, will 'scapegoat' the leader(s). This comes partly from a history of not having power or responsibility for ourselves, and therefore investing all that power in teachers, parents and community leaders. Taking responsibility can be a painful process, and participants may unthinkingly, or sometimes angrily, place all responsibility with you, especially for something they perceive as going 'wrong', for example, a bad performance. If you are working alone, this is particularly difficult, and it is important not to internalise the blame as a criticism of you, but to see it as a natural process of the group. Employ the support mechanisms outlined above, be aware that it will probably happen at some stage and have some strategies and exercises ready for dealing with it. Make it clear that you are the facilitator – you are responsible for yourself and your work – but that equally they are responsible for theirs. This may involve a time when they need to reinvestigate the groundrules, but they will learn more from undertaking this process. The stock response to a transgression would be exclusion or punishment but this is a space to try something different.

Once the group have moved through the resentment and scapegoating and renegotiated their position, bring all of you together with some games or a relaxation session and move on (*see also* Groundrules, Unit One).

HOW TO STRUCTURE A WORKSHOP

Preparation is crucial in running a successful workshop, especially when you start out. You can always adapt your plan in response to the group once the workshop is underway.

Preparation:

- Aims – why are you doing it?
- Objectives – how will you do it?
- Numbers – how many do you expect? What if they don't all turn up?
- Time – how long is the session? How long is each section?
- Materials – do you need to take anything with you?
- The group – who are they and why are they doing this?
- Concerns – do you have any particular concerns about the space, or the group?
- Any possible responses?
- Co-facilitation – who will lead which section?

The minimum number you need for a workshop is two, or four if you want to work in two groups. The maximum for an individual facilitator is about 15, depending on age, but there may be times, usually in schools, when you deal with more. If you are working in a school and are not a trained teacher yourself, there must be a teacher with you by law. They can then also support you.

An ideal length of time for a session is an hour and a half. One hour is OK, but not quite enough (except with younger groups when it is ideal), and two hours means people will start to get tired and lose concentration towards the end. However, neither are impossible. The more workshops you do, the easier it becomes as you gain experience. It is very important to reflect and evaluate – how can you improve your working practice?

There are five elements to a workshop which can be applied to any length of session, and should aim to include whole group work, pairs work and small group work:

- Warm-Up
- Informing the Drama
- Creating the Drama
- Evaluation
- Reflection/Closing.

The Warm-Up: games and exercises that bring the group together for this session, even if they know each other.

Informing the Drama: games and exercises geared to the theme and form of the workshop that will provide a core knowledge for the group to work with for that session, and inform the drama. It is a jumping-off point, so that they are not starting from 'cold'. You may use pairs work, or sharing experiences in small groups, or other triggers.

Creating the Drama: the bulk of the workshop session. The group can use images or scenes, and they will be working in smaller groups to create their own work and experience the excitement of actually doing drama.

Evaluation: this is when they can show their pieces to each other and evaluate them through giving feedback. It also allows time for affirmation of the work to take place.

Reflection/Closing: a reflection on the day's session – not necessary for every single session through the day, but definitely at the end of the day or week – plus a wind-down exercise or game for relaxation.

EXAMPLE WORKSHOPS
The games and exercises described here are all to be found in this manual.

Example Workshop One
An introductory workshop on homelessness for a new group of young homeless people, some with, some without drama experience.

Time:	Two hours
Number in Group:	20
Materials:	Flipchart, pen
Aims:	To engage the group in an active exploration of homelessness and to bring the group together using games, exercises and drama.
Warm-Up:	Games – one or two ice breakers, light and livelies such as The Sun Shines On, Tag, Person to Person, Mill, Grab and Tab etc. (10 minutes).
Informing the Drama:	Brainstorm on 'homelessness' with the whole group. Break into smaller groups, select a word, make an image of it and share these images with the rest of the group.

In pairs, tell personal stories of homelessness, bring back to the main group and make a list of associated words (40 minutes).

Creating Drama: Get into groups. In these groups, make further images, then either analyse them or bring them to life. Inform the drama further by highlighting the central character's story and discussing what their motivation is (40 minutes).

Evaluation: Show the pieces, general feedback (15 minutes).

Reflection/Closing: Gathering; a closing (see Closings, Unit One) (5–10 minutes).

Example Workshop Two

A group with some experience of drama, who have already done some work together.

Time: One and a half hours

Number in Group: 10

Materials: Newspapers

Aim: To develop the group's skills in creating educational theatre using facts as the starting point to create the drama.

Warm-Up: Mill, Grab and Tab or other drama based game, linked to theme (10 minutes).

Informing the Drama: Exercise using newspaper captions creating 'photos' or other drama work. Share with the whole group.

You could also brainstorm possible drama styles to use in creating the work, such as horror, western etc. (10 minutes).

Creating the Drama: Move on to using newspaper stories as triggers for scenes. You could build the scenes using three images of the beginning, middle and end of the story (40 minutes).

Evaluation: Show scenes and listen to feedback from group on what worked well and what needed improvement (20 minutes).

Reflection/Closing: Wind down; Link Tag (5–10 minutes).

Example Workshop Three

A small group, very unsure of themselves, with no drama experience and sporadic attendance.

Time:	One hour
Number in Group:	4 or 5
Materials:	Newspaper headlines, flipchart, pen.
Aims:	To interest the group enough to come again; to offer a space to be creative and share experiences; to build trust through use of games and drama exercises.
Warm-Up:	The Sun Shines On, Points of Contact, Share the Fact games or Touch Three Things (5–10 minutes).
Informing the Drama:	Brainstorm the theme as a whole group, encouraging everyone to contribute. Use image work (or 'photos' or 'freezeframe') as a safe way to begin drama, and explore issues (15 minutes).
Creating the Drama:	Give starting points for an improvisation in two smaller groups. These starting points could be newspaper headlines, or sentences worked out in advance; or they could build characters as a group, starting from pictures or objects. It is a good idea to build scenes, using frozen pictures of the beginning, middle and end of a story; use Touch and Tell, then think of one sentence for each picture. Go round and help the groups create what they want to say (20 minutes).
Evaluation:	Each group shows their work to the other group, and asks some questions about the pieces (10–15 minutes).
Reflection/Closing:	A go-round (5 minutes).

These are basic workshop outlines to help you to start planning your own. As you grow more confident, you will find your own style emerging, and you may want to adapt these structures.

UNIT ONE

THE FIRST STEPS

The first steps towards *the leap* are making the decision to move forward and finding the courage to leave behind our existing way of life. We must then make preparations, so that *the leap* can take place on solid ground.

Unit One: Preparation

UNIT GUIDE

Introduction
Ready: Recruitment
Steady: The Introductory Workshop
Go: Creating a Safe Space
Games
Groundrules
Group Work
Closings
Action Research

INTRODUCTION

The first steps require thorough planning, a solid groundwork to prepare for the leap. This unit will help you to think about recruiting a group, interesting them in a project and creating a safe space where the work can take place, as well as starting the research in order to explore the issue.

Ready, steady, go!

READY: RECRUITMENT

- Are you ready to start your theatre project?
- Do you have the funding?
- Do you have a good space to work in?
- Do you have support from other colleagues in your work place?

If the answers to the above questions are *yes,* then keep going!

Working with an Established Group

You may be working with a group of young people in a youth club, a school, a care unit or a homeless hostel who know each other and meet regularly. Ideally the interest and the ideas for the project should come from them. What do they want to achieve? Is it feasible? If they are in control of deciding on the theme and how/when the project will take place, then the process of empowerment has already begun. Even if attendance is obligatory, try to ensure that some aspect of choice is integrated into the setting up of the project, so a conscious decision has been made by those participating. Along with a greater sense of ownership, this will foster greater investment in the project's success and therefore greater commitment, energy and enthusiasm. Ask the group: what are the four or five most important issues for them? Which ones would they most like to explore? These first steps are crucial in making *the leap* a valuable and rewarding experience. However, don't be put off by an apparent lack of interest – they may need more input (including suggestions from you and a 'taster' session) to get motivated and begin to recognise the potential benefits a project might have. Take the time to develop their ideas and make sure that the challenge set is achievable to avoid disappointment.

Recruiting a Group (see also Equal Opportunities Policy, Practicalities)

In the case of Leap, there is no pre-established group. However, the project structure and theme are set prior to recruiting a group, drawing on recommendations from past projects. It is important when recruiting a group to have this clear structure to offer, which is defined enough to support participants' needs but flexible enough to allow their input. You may wish to decide on the theme once the group is established. However, Leap's experience of deciding the theme in advance has proved successful over the years. It attracts potential participants who are interested in a specific issue, provides an immediate focus for the group and enables the project workers to undertake background research before the project officially starts.

Have you decided who the project is for? Is your target group young homeless people or young offenders, school leavers or refugees? Once you have identified this, it is important to ensure that you reach them through appropriate recruitment. This process can in itself prove to be difficult. This applies especially if you are targeting young people who are very isolated and lack confidence. How successful you are at involving them depends on whether the recruitment process and the project itself responds to their interests and needs. A few recommendations follow to maximise successful recruitment.

> *Research:* Get to know your target group. Find out where they spend time, what their interests are, any religious and cultural factors which will affect their participation etc.

Time: Do not underestimate the time needed to undertake outreach and recruitment. Plan enough time into your schedule.

Raise the Profile: Play up the benefits of the project and be sure to key into aspects which will appeal to your target group, for example, award a certificate, or highlight the tour.

Leaflets/Flyers: Make sure you have plenty of leaflets visible where your target group spends time, for example, in a homeless hostel or a job centre. They should be bright and colourful, drawing on popular culture and easy to read. Make sure times, dates, and venue details are clear.

Figure 1.1 Distributing flyers

Face to Face: Attend drop-in centres and youth clubs and chat to young people there, get to know them and let them get to know you.

Figure 1.2 'Can I interest you in a project?'

Adverts: Place adverts in local newspapers and magazines which young people are likely to read, such as *The Voice*, *The Big Issue*, *Time Out*. Also use popular radio stations such as Kiss FM.

Figure 1.3 Grandma listens out

Referrals: Get other workers on your side – they can be doing your recruitment for you if they speak highly of your project to the young people they work with.

Track Record: If you have undertaken successful project work before, use any materials produced, such as photos, video material and articles, to validate the success of your work. Get another young person to talk about their experience – their opinion counts.

Introductory Workshop: (*see* Steady section below): Make sure your introductory workshop is held in an accessible space and at an appropriate time. Ensure that the space does not in itself put people off, for example a room in a jobcentre.

Written Outline: It is useful to offer a written outline of the project, detailing training elements, so that potential participants have a detailed understanding of the whole project.

These recommendations do not guarantee participation, but they will ensure that the recruitment process does not let you down. Ultimately, an exciting, challenging and accessible project is the best recruitment tool.

STEADY: THE INTRODUCTORY WORKSHOP
Facilitator's Preparation

Assuming you have undertaken the initial stages of the recruitment process, you now need to plan a preparation time when you can develop a working relationship with your co-worker, and plan your first section of training. If the theme has been decided beforehand, you can also use this time to research the issues and collate information.

> *Visits:* Visits to, and telephone conversations with, voluntary and statutory agencies will offer expert insight into the work, and information on the issues you aim to cover. They may be able to suggest reading material and videos to watch. You can also ask them to come and speak to the group, to give a personal account of their work.

> *Planning and Preparation of Materials:* Use this time to agree aims and objectives, plan introductory workshops, invite speakers, watch documentary material and plan the first few training days.

> *Introductory Workshop:* At Leap, we offer a taster of the work, allowing potential participants to make an informed choice about this next step. Is this the right project for them? Will they be able to make the commitment required, whether this is for one evening a week, two days a week, or three months full-time?

The introductory workshop offers a space to actively explore some of these questions, and a chance to informally discuss the realities of taking part in devising a show, performing and perhaps touring a piece of theatre. However short or long the project is, it is vital to ensure that the participants understand what is required of them on this particular piece of work, and what they will gain by taking part. Are they ready to take this step?

A more detailed breakdown of the structure of a workshop is given in The Facilitator's Guide above, but the important elements of an introductory workshop are:

- an introduction to the aims and structure of the project
- a practical taster of the issues and techniques involved
- a question and answer session with the whole group following the taster

- a one-to-one informal interview of about 15 minutes with one of the facilitators, where individual concerns can be discussed and the suitability of potential participants can be assessed.

The aim of the introductory workshop is to interest people in the project, and it needs to be as open and informative as possible, so that potential participants can make an informed choice. This also means that they are playing an active role right from the start.

Quotes from previous participants on why they attended the introductory workshop:

- 'I hoped that this project would create positive change and hope'
- 'They showed me a number of leaflets; I saw most of myself in the turquoise one'
- 'At the time I was really looking for a directional opportunity. Leap seemed ideal'
- 'I didn't know what else to do; my life was at a complete standstill'
- 'The chance to develop creatively and raise awareness of issues I care greatly about'
- 'I received a leaflet from New Horizon, and I met a few Leap members there too'
- 'I wanted to know more, learn new skills and meet new people'
- 'For self-development'
- 'A personal challenge to see if I could really do it'.

Selection: Whilst aiming largely for self-selection, inevitably there may be more potential participants than there are places, and the demands of the project are not suitable for everyone. At Leap one of the most important elements of a project is to create a balanced group whose membership is representative of a cross-section of the community in which we live in terms of ethnicity, gender, ability and life experience. Our experience shows that this deliberate mixture of different experiences and backgrounds creates a dynamic process of growth and learning for all participants and trainers involved. Where selection is necessary, we recruit a group on this basis. There are a maximum number of 14 places on each project, which is a good group size, and allows for one or two dropping out. Once the selection has been made, we contact each young person by phone and/or letter to discuss why we have decided not to offer them a place or to invite them to join the project. When these recruitment steps have been taken, you're ready to go!

GO: CREATING A SAFE SPACE

This section looks primarily at the first few days/weeks of the project when the foundations of the recruitment process can be built on to transform your group into a cohesive unit. There are two primary factors which need to be considered in this process.

Group Identity

Unless your group already know each other prior to the project, time must be spent fostering a sense of 'the group' whereby barriers are broken down, they share common ideas, concerns and goals and individuals gain a sense of belonging. This cohesion allows for greater communication, cooperation and trust between group members, creating a safe space within which members are free to express their differences and individuality without fear of exclusion. The use of the circle in games and group work is very important in facilitating a positive identity for the group. It deepens the notion of equality existing between group members and provides a forum for safe and structured debate to flourish. This positive sense of identity can develop a feeling of confidence which many young people do not possess. It can also enhance the shared vision of the theatre piece, creating a powerful and real performance.

Group Ownership

For the identity of the group to be one of power, the group needs to have control over the decision-making process and experience the responsibility which exists with this role. Through the use of games, exercises, group work and discussion, you can establish a way of working which involves participants actively in the running of the group. As a facilitator, you will be planning the process in advance, but it is important that these structures that you set in place are made explicit to the group. For example, it is good practice to highlight why you have chosen a certain activity and offer the group a chance to reflect on that decision. This serves to include them in the process and increases their understanding of the need for careful and well thought-out planning.

The next part of this unit provides you with the practical material which will give you the tools to implement the above. Some activities, for example, name games and the group contract, are specific to the beginning of the project, whilst other activities, for example, the energisers and the closings, can be used throughout the whole of your training, to start and end sessions and develop the group's skills.

GAMES

When we are given 'permission to play' it can be an exhilarating experience, tapping into the energy we had as children. Games can serve several purposes: they can release emotional and physical energy; increase mobility, coordination and balance; break down inhibitions; increase self-awareness and discovery; build relationships; develop the group; create a common vocabulary; and, of course, they can be fun!

Ice Breakers

A selection of group games to break down barriers, share information, encourage safe physical contact and have fun.

1. Three Name Games

Time:	10 minutes each
Materials:	for b) three bean bags
	for c) paper and marker pen, chairs
Number in Group:	Minimum of 3/Maximum of 15
Aim:	A choice of three games for group members to learn each other's names in an active way.

(a) Name and Number
DIRECTIONS:
Ask the group to stand in a circle and go round saying their names.

Give each person a number (one upwards) and ask the group to move around the room. When you call out number one, that person says their name and an activity they like doing that begins with the same letter as their name, which they then mime, for example, 'My name is Jenny and I like jumping'.

The group then repeats the sentence and mimes the action, for example, 'This is Jenny and she likes jumping'. Repeat this through the numbers, until the whole group has introduced themselves.

DEVELOPMENT:
Repeat the whole game at twice the speed, varying the order of the numbers you call out. Bring the group back together into a circle and facilitate one final round of name and activity in unison at high speed.

(b) Name Balls
DIRECTIONS:
Ask the group to stand in a circle and throw a ball to each other. As people throw the ball they call out their own name. Change the instruction to saying

the name of the person you are throwing the ball to and not your own name. Introduce another ball and if the group are managing well, introduce a third ball.

You can slow the game down or finish it subtly by taking away the balls as you catch them.

DEVELOPMENT:

Ask people to walk around the room whilst playing.

NOTE:

Some group members may not be confident catching a ball. Make sure that the emphasis is not on being able to catch, but on sharing names.

(c) Name on Paper

DIRECTIONS:

Ask the group to sit in a circle. Put a large sheet of paper and a marker pen in the centre. Ask group members, one by one, to volunteer to write down their own name and then speak to the group about it, such as, what it means, if they have a nickname they prefer, a story connected to it etc. Continue until everyone has shared their name.

NOTE:

Encourage everyone to say something about their name even if it is whether they like it or not.

2. Three Fact Games (see also Trust Games, Unit One)

Time:	10–15 minutes each
Materials:	(for (c)) chairs
Number in Group:	Minimum of 6
Aim:	A choice of three safe and fun ways to share personal information and build trust.

(a) Share Three Facts

DIRECTIONS:

Give the group two minutes to move around the room, greeting other group members one-to-one and sharing their names and three facts about themselves with as many people as possible. Encourage the group to vary the facts with the different people and to listen to the facts they are being told as well.

When the time is up, gather group members and ask them to call out the facts they heard without revealing the name of the person whose fact it is. In this way, the anonymous facts become shared information without individuals having to say them to the whole group at once.

VARIATIONS:

Ask the group to get into pairs and label each other A and B. Give A two minutes to tell B about themselves. B listens and then has two minutes to tell A about themselves.

Reconvene the group into a circle and invite each of the pairs to introduce their partners to the group by offering three facts about them that they have learnt.

NOTE:

Remind the group to take responsibility for the information they volunteer to share.

(b) Act the Fact

DIRECTIONS:

Ask the group to move around the room. Ask people to get into groups of a certain number: twos, threes, fours etc. In their groups they have to decide on something they have in common with each other and then act it out, without saying it, for example, they all enjoy playing football.

When all the groups have prepared something, ask them to 'act their fact' for the other groups to guess. Repeat with different size groups.

VARIATIONS:

Instead of calling out the size of the group, this time call out a subject that people might have in common, for example, 'Get into groups with people who have the same colour toothbrush as you'.

Go round quickly hearing what each group's common theme is. You can start with superficial themes and deepen the nature of the game by calling out a riskier theme, if appropriate.

DEVELOPMENTS:

Ask the group to share their common theme in silence, through mime.

NOTE:

Stress that it is all right if one person is unable to find others who share the same thing in common and that they can make a group on their own.

(c) The Sun Shines On

DIRECTIONS:

The group sits on chairs in a circle, with one chair short. One person stands in the middle, who wants a seat. They say 'The sun shines on everyone who...' and then say something true about themselves, such as 'has blue eyes', or 'likes swimming'.

If this is true of anyone else in the circle, they also have to move to another seat, but they cannot move to the seat next to them, or return to their own seat.

DEVELOPMENT:

The level of information being shared can be deepened, for example to political beliefs, or linked to the theme, such as drug use, or the shared concerns of a group, such as unemployment.

NOTES:

Ensure the exercise is built gradually, from 'safe' information, to more personal information.

In the excitement, people can get boisterous, so ensure care is taken in crossing the circle.

3. Person to Person (see also Trust Games, Cooperation Games, Unit One)

    Time: 10–15 minutes

    Number in Group: Minimum of 6

    Aim: A whole group/pairs game, offering a safe way of breaking down physical barriers, and therefore enhancing trust within the group.

DIRECTIONS:

Ask the whole group to move around the room, perhaps varying speed and mood. When you call out 'person to person' everyone finds a partner. Then call out different parts of the body for the partners to touch, for example, hand to hand, little finger to thumb, foot to back. Each point of contact must be held while the next is added, building up three or four, creating some interesting contortions!

When you call out 'move around', they break and move around until you call 'person to person' again, when they find a new partner.

Repeat three or four times, until the group have mixed well.

DEVELOPMENT:

Build the exercise in fours then eights etc. until the whole group is touching one another.

NOTES:

This exercise needs care in setting up, making sure that the points of contact are appropriate, and that people don't abuse the physical contact involved.

4. Points of Contact (see also Cooperation Games, Unit One)

    Time: 10 minutes

    Number in Group: Minimum of 6

Aim: Cooperative problem solving, also allowing safe physical contact, and therefore building trust.

DIRECTIONS:

Ask everyone to move around the room, and then ask people to get into groups of a certain number: twos, threes, fours etc. Call out a number of points of contact that each group has to make with the floor, where one foot or one elbow, for example, equals one point of contact. Backs, bottoms, heads and each knee all count as one point. The group must work cooperatively to achieve this, perhaps lifting each other up, or giving piggy backs.

Repeat three or four times, getting people into different size groups, and varying the number of points of contact. Move around the groups affirming when they have achieved the number so they are not holding uncomfortable positions for long.

NOTES:

The number of points of contact can be made increasingly difficult. Sometimes a group may get stuck, and not see a solution, and so need some suggestions.

Ensure that people move around and work in different groups, and in small and large groups. End as a whole group, all working cooperatively.

Figure 1.4 Points of Contact

Light and Livelies/Energisers

A selection of active games that can be used to raise energy levels first thing in the morning, after a break, or as a release after a concentrated period of work.

Care needs to be taken, so that people do not hurt each other unintentionally in the excitement, particularly with younger groups.

The length of each game usually depends on the size of the group.

1. Touch Three Things (see also Ice Breaker Games, Unit One)

Time:	5–10 minutes
Number in Group:	Minimum of 3
Aim:	A simple whole group game to raise energy levels, involving running around.

DIRECTIONS:

Gather the group in the middle of the room. Call out three things that each person must touch, in any order. When you call 'Go' they then race each other to do this and get back to the starting point. The last one back calls the next three things.

Examples: a radiator, something blue, something cold.

DEVELOPMENT:

The game could be themed to the subject of the workshop, touching, for example, three dangerous things.

2. Bums on Seats

Time:	10 minutes
Materials:	Chairs
Number in Group:	Minimum of 8
Aim:	A fun energiser requiring cooperation by the whole group.

DIRECTIONS:

Everyone sits down on chairs, facing inwards, with one chair vacant. One person stands in the middle, with the aim of getting the free seat, but the group try and prevent them by each person moving quickly round to the seat next to them. This creates a wave-like effect, that means the vacant seat 'moves' round the circle.

When they manage to get to the seat, one other person will naturally be displaced, and they become the new person in the middle, and so the game continues.

NOTE:

Very energetic and possibly boisterous.

3. Tag Games (see also Ice Breakers, Unit One)

    Time: 5–10 minutes each game

    Number in Group: Minimum of 3, except for (g) which needs minimum of 6

    Aim: A selection of running around games, to energise the whole group.

DIRECTIONS:

(a) Tag: One person is 'it', and tries to catch the others. If someone is caught, they become the new 'it'. The games that follow are variations on this.

(b) Mirror Tag: When someone is caught, they must freeze in an interesting position. They can only be freed by someone else mirroring their position, and counting to three. While someone is mirroring them, they are immune from being caught. Swap around the person who is 'it'.

(c) Animal Tag: The person who is 'it' has to move round like an animal, making animal noises. When they catch someone, the new 'it' becomes a different animal.

(d) Singing Tag: The person who is 'it' has to sing while they are chasing the others. Each time someone is caught and becomes the new 'it', they sing a different song.

(e) Stuck in the Mud Tag: When someone is caught, they become 'stuck in the mud', frozen with their legs apart. They can only be freed if someone else crawls through their legs. While someone is crawling through, they are immune from being caught. Swap around the new 'it'.

(f) Link Tag: A good game for bringing people back together as a whole group. One person starts off as 'it', and when they catch someone, they link arms and continue to be 'it'. When they catch someone else, they also link on, and so on until the whole group is linked together.

(g) Cat and Mouse: The group links arms in pairs and one person puts their arm outstretched to the side, while the other puts their hand on their hip forming a 'link' arm. One pair is given the roles of cat (chaser) and mouse (chased).

The person who is the cat chases the mouse, who is only safe when s/he catches on to the link arm of another pair. This then releases the other person, with the outstretched arm, who becomes the new mouse and is chased by the cat. If the cat catches the mouse, they swap roles.

4. Bomb and Shield

Time:	10 minutes
Number in Group:	Minimum of 4
Aim:	A whole group energiser, that can be linked to the theme of the workshop.

DIRECTIONS:

Ask everyone to decide on one person in the group who is their 'bomb' for the purposes of this game. When you say 'go', everyone must try and get as far away from their 'bomb' as possible within the room. Call out 'freeze'.

Next, everyone decides on a 'shield', who must be between them and their bomb for protection. On 'go', everyone must try and stay protected and when their shield or bomb moves, they must move to keep protected. Call out 'freeze'.

FEEDBACK AND DISCUSSION:

On freezing the game again, ask people to look at where they are in relation to their bomb and the shield. If the bomb exploded now, would they be protected? How might the game relate to a theme, such as dependency or drugs? This feedback work could be done in pairs or as a whole group.

DEVELOPMENT:

If relating the game to a theme, such as bullying, ask the group to select their bomb thinking of them as a bully for the purposes of this game. Then ask them to think about what or who might be the shield from this bully – a teacher? A friend?

Feedback and discuss at the end of the game. Would the shield be effective? If so, for how long? Will the shield always be there?

NOTE:

Ensure that everyone understands that the 'bomb' is for the purposes of the game only!

5. Greet, Argue and Make Up

Time:	10–15 minutes
Number in Group:	Minimum of 4
Aim:	A drama-based game in pairs, building energy levels.

DIRECTIONS:

Ask everyone to walk around the room, and then find a partner.

They greet this partner as if they were a long-lost friend, hugging them, asking how they are etc. When you call 'stop', they move off round the room again.

Ask them to meet a new partner, and have a huge argument with this new 'character'. Call 'stop', and they move off around the room again.

Finally, ask them to find a third partner and make up the 'argument', until you call 'finish'.

Then repeat the exercise, this time asking them to exaggerate the level of emotion in each encounter; and then repeat it once more, exaggerating the energy levels even more, until it is completely over the top, with people begging on their knees for forgiveness.

FEEDBACK AND DISCUSSION:
Allow some time at the end of this game for people to comment informally to each other.

NOTES:
This game is a tremendous energy releaser, especially for a reserved group. It is also good to play when/if your group are feeling frustrated/angry with each other, allowing them to release that anger in a safe and indirect way.

6. Dangerous Places

Time:	10 minutes
Number in Group:	Minimum of 3
Aim:	An imaginative energiser that can be linked to a themed workshop.

DIRECTIONS:
Tell the group to think of a 'dangerous place' within the room, then ask them to move around the space.

When you call out 'dangerous places', they must run to the place they selected and position themselves by it, indicating why it might be dangerous.

Go round the group, asking each person what is dangerous about that place, and why, for example, 'I might burn myself on this radiator'.

Build the game by playing once or twice, with increasing speed and energy, and with the places becoming life-threatening, for example, 'the roof might fall in on me' or 'there might be an earthquake and the floor cave in.'

FEEDBACK AND DISCUSSION:
What is attractive about danger? How might this link to crime/drugs?

Concentration Games

A selection of games which can be used to focus your group, prior to a main exercise which demands concentration. The different games have different energy levels, which can be used as appropriate with your group and the activity you plan to undertake.

1. Wink Murder

Time:	10–15 minutes
Number in Group:	Minimum of 6
Aim:	To focus and calm your group. Based on the children's game.

DIRECTIONS:

Ask the group to sit in a circle and close their eyes.

You go round the outside of the circle and tap one person on the shoulder, who then becomes the murderer.

Everyone opens their eyes and are informed that there is a murderer among them and if they are winked at, they have been killed and must wait ten seconds before acting out a horrendous death. The murderer aims to kill as many group members as possible without being found out.

The group aims to discover who the murderer is.

When someone thinks they know, they put their hand up and make a guess. If they are right, the game ends, if not, they die and the game continues without them.

VARIATIONS:

- Rather than the group members guessing, select a detective when you select the murderer, who sits in the centre of the circle and has three guesses to find the murderer.

- If a higher energy level is needed, play the game walking around the room with a detective standing to one side.

2. Lawyer

Time:	10 minutes
Number in Group:	Minimum of 6
Aim:	A concentration game which requires mental speed and tactics to succeed.

DIRECTIONS:

Tell the group to sit on chairs in a circle, with one less chair than there are people.

Ask for a volunteer to stand in the centre of the circle and take on the role of the 'detective', asking group members questions about something, such as an invented incident, or what they have been doing. However, the group member cannot answer, and their 'lawyer' who is the person sitting to the left of them must answer instead, while the detective tries to catch people out. If the person answers accidentally or if their lawyer does not respond, they become the detective.

DEVELOPMENT:

To make it more difficult the lawyer could be the person sitting two seats to the left.

NOTE:

Encourage the detective to try different strategies to catch the group members out.

3. Are You Ready? (see also Name Games, Unit One)

Time: 10–15 minutes

Number in Group: Minimum of 5

Aim: A concentration game which develops the rhythmic skills of the participants.

DIRECTIONS:

Ask the group to sit on chairs in a circle and label them from one upwards. Begin a rhythm to a beat of four.

On one: slap hands on thighs

On two: clap hands

On three: click with the left hand

On four: click with the right hand.

Get everyone doing this rhythm together at a speed which is comfortable. Explain that while everyone keeps doing the rhythm, number one starts and on the next left hand click says their number and then on the next right hand click, another random number. The person who is that number then repeats their number on the left hand click and says another random number on the right hand click, for example, 1 to 7, 7 to 3, 3 to 6 etc... Continue this until someone makes a mistake at which point they are out and their number disappears. From now on no one can pass to this number and if someone does, they are also out. The game ends when only a few people are left.

Remember, you cannot pass back to the number who just passed to you.

If you wish, you can start the game using the left and right click to say:

Concentration

Are you ready?

If so

Let's go!

VARIATIONS:

Use group members' names instead of numbers or a theme such as types of fruit.

NOTES:

You can adjust the speed depending on the competence of your group. Be aware that some people can find a rhythm very hard.

4. Zip Zap Boing (see also Cooperation Games, Unit One)

Time: 10 minutes

Number in Group: Minimum of 4

Aim: To focus and energise your group.

DIRECTIONS:

Ask the group to stand in a circle. Explain that you have a ball of energy in your hands which can pass around the room as a clap. Introduce the first mode of travel: a zip, which is a clap passed around the circle in one direction. As you pass the clap you say 'zip!'

Do a few rounds of this until the group are fast and energetic. Then introduce a zap; this is passed across the circle from one person to another, by pointing the clap in their direction whilst saying 'zap'.

Do a few 'zap' rounds and then introduce the third mode of travel, the 'boing' which reflects the 'zip' or 'zap' back to the person who sent it. The person says 'boing' and holds up both hands as if to push back the 'zip' or 'zap'. If a 'zip' is 'boinged' the person can 'zip' in the other direction or 'zap'.

Try using all three modes of travel and continue, increasing speed and energy as appropriate.

DEVELOPMENTS:

You can add some new rules to the game to maximise the energy:

- 'I throw', whereby one person throws the energy ball into the middle of the circle, leaving it open for anyone to say 'I take' and restart the 'zip'/'zap' around the circle. If two people say 'I take' together, there is usually one who sustains the next 'zip'/'zap'.

- 'I run', which instructs the group to run randomly around the circle until the person who said it taps someone on the shoulder who reforms the circle by passing a 'zip'.

NOTES:

If you play this game regularly with your group they can make up their own new rules. This game is great played silently without calling out the 'zip', 'zap' or 'boing' prior to a performance to energise and gel the group but not disturb the audience. (*see also* Pre-Performance/Energiser, Unit Four.)

5. Jailbreak

Time:	15 minutes
Materials:	Chairs
Number in Group:	Minimum of 5
Aim:	A high energy concentration game with the whole group.

DIRECTIONS:

Set up a circle of chairs and ask the equivalent number of group members to stand a foot behind the chairs, hands to their sides. They are the 'wardens'. Other group members sit in the chairs, leaving at least three of the chairs empty. They are the 'prisoners'. Therefore, three of the wardens have no prisoners. In order to get prisoners, they must wink at another prisoner who then has to 'escape' their chair and run to the new chair. However, each warden is guarding their prisoner and can prevent an escape by tapping the prisoner on her/his back before they move out of reach. The prisoner then has to stay with the present warden.

Repeat game and swap over some of the prisoners and wardens.

FEEDBACK AND DISCUSSION:

How did it feel being a prisoner? A warden? How many of the prisoners escaped? Most group members who played prisoners will put up their hands at this question, but you can ask them where they actually escaped to. What other situations could you apply this game to?

NOTE:

Decide in advance how many chairs you need to set up, depending on the size of your group.

Trust Games

The existence of trust within a group is of great importance, allowing individuals the safety to speak and move freely without fear of betrayal or ridicule. For young people whose trust has been broken by family, friends or society, it can be difficult to trust people. However, without this, the group process is undermined.

The following selection of games allow participants to develop physical trust of each other. It is important that personal choice and responsibility is taken and participation is not forced.

1. Three Blind Mice

Time:	10 minutes each
Number in Group:	Minimum of 4
Aim:	To develop mutual trust within the group. To provide participants with the experience of physically trusting someone else and being entrusted with the responsibility of someone else's safety.

(a) Blind Leading
DIRECTIONS:

Ask everyone to find a partner and label each other A and B.

A closes her/his eyes and B gently takes A's hand, so that there is a point of contact between them. In silence, B moves A around the room, taking care not to bump into anyone or anything. Only if B feels that A is OK, should she/he speed up, and explore the possibilities more, always putting A's safety first. After a few minutes, B brings A to a halt. Change round, so that A is leading B. Using her/his experience of the game, A can now lead B around the room. Bring to a halt.

FEEDBACK AND DISCUSSION:

Allow the pair time to feedback to each other their experience of the exercise. Bring the whole group together. What was it like being led? What was it like leading? Which did participants feel more comfortable with? Why?

(b) Animal Noises
DIRECTIONS:

This time, in pairs, lead each other by sound and not touch. In each pair choose an animal sound. B, standing about a metre in front of A, leads A around the room by making that sound. A must follow the direction of the sound and be still when no sound is heard. If B is confident that A is feeling safe, B can move further away, lessen the continuity of the sound, decrease the volume, etc... Bring the pair to a halt and swap A and B. Ask them to use the same or a different sound.

FEEDBACK AND DISCUSSION:

Allow the pair time to feedback together, then bring the whole group together. Compare this experience to the last one. Was touch or sound more preferable? Why? Were group members put off by other sounds? If not, why not?

(c) Imaginary Journey
DIRECTIONS:

In pairs, A closes her/his eyes and B, holding A's hand, takes A on an imaginary journey. Using sound and objects, B can create an environment for A to travel through, climbing over chairs, under tables etc., always making sure that A is safe. Bring the journey to an end. Swap roles.

FEEDBACK AND DISCUSSION:

Let the pair feedback to each other. Bring the whole group together. Ask members to highlight what were the best and worst moments of the journey and why? Did they feel safe? If so, why? If not, why not?

NOTES:

When working with a younger group, you may need to introduce a narrative to (a) and (b) to enhance the sense of play and use the imagination. For example, (a) could be described as a firefighter helping a person to safety from a fire; (b) could be a farmer looking for her/his animals.

Ensure that in all three variations, the trust is not broken by participants laughing or being silly. Reiterate the importance of caring for your partner.

2. Hands Off

Time:	10 minutes
Number in Group:	Minimum of 4
Aim:	To develop participants' sensory awareness, sensitivity to each other and trust.

DIRECTIONS:

Ask group members to find a partner and label each other A and B. Ask both partners to take off any rings or watches they are wearing. A closes her/his eyes and spends a minute gently feeling B's hands – the size, the shape, length of nails, texture etc. Then B moves away from A and stands in a new place. A tries to refind her/his partner with her/his eyes closed by touching the hands of people whom she/he meets on the way. When A finds B, swap over.

DEVELOPMENT:

If the group feels comfortable with each other, use faces not hands.

FEEDBACK AND DISCUSSION:

Let the pair feedback to each other, then bring the whole group together and hear observations from group members reflecting on the exercise. How did people feel when they found their partner? Was it easy to recognise hands?

NOTES:

Make sure you and other 'sighted' participants are there to prevent those with their eyes shut from walking into walls. You may want to help direct a few people who are struggling to find their partner.

3. Trust Circles

Time:	15 minutes each
Number in Group:	for a) Minimum of 2
	for b) Minimum of 5
	for c) Minimum of 6
Aim:	Three exercises to encourage caring, support and trust on a one-to-one, small group and whole group level.

(a) One to One:
DIRECTIONS:

Everyone finds a partner who is roughly the same size as them, and labels themselves A and B. B stands approximately one foot behind A. B is facing A, with one foot behind the other and her/his arms up, ready to catch A. When A is ready, she/he falls back into B's arms. A must use her/his feet as a pivot, keeping the body straight and both arms by her/his side. Repeat this a few times, increasing the gap between A and B, so the fall is further. Swap roles.

FEEDBACK AND DISCUSSION:

Allow time for pairs to feedback to each other how it felt falling back and catching.

(b) Small Group Trust
DIRECTIONS:

Get into groups of at least five participants, standing in a circle. Ask for a volunteer to stand in the centre of the circle with their eyes closed and their hands either by their side or across their chest. The rest of the group stand with one foot behind the other so they can support the body weight of the volunteer. When ready, ask the volunteer to let themself fall, pivoting from their feet, allowing the group to move him/her back and forth around the circle. If the volunteer feels relaxed and confident, then widen the circle; if the volunteer is nervous, come closer in. Swap after a few minutes. Give everyone the opportunity to be in the centre.

FEEDBACK AND DISCUSSION:

Offer the participants the opportunity to voice their experience of this exercise.

NOTES:

If not taken seriously, this exercise can break down trust in a group. Reiterate the importance of maintaining silence to focus the exercise and that the aim is to support the central person and not to throw/push them around. Use your own knowledge of your group to measure how they will approach this exercise and use it or don't use it accordingly.

(c) Large Group Trust
DIRECTIONS:

Gather the group into a large circle. Ask for a volunteer to shut their eyes and set off walking across the circle. When they reach the other side, the person nearest them gently stops them and turns them around to continue in a different direction. After a number of journeys, bring this person to a halt and invite a new volunteer to take part. Offer everyone the opportunity to try this. Stress the importance of the whole group as participants on someone else's journey.

FEEDBACK AND DISCUSSION:

Depending on the size of the group, invite short feedback from each person after they have had a go. This is a good time to voice immediate feelings/responses to the experience.

4. Three Ways to Fall

Time:	15–20 minutes
Number in Group:	Minimum of 8
Aim:	To deepen the already established trust of a group and take personal risks within a safe framework.

(a) Sky High
DIRECTIONS:

A volunteer lies on the floor and other group members gather around and together pick up the person and raise them horizontally above their heads. Making sure the person is safe, walk off as a group, carrying the person around the room. After one or two minutes, stop and carefully lower the person to the ground. Offer this opportunity to each group member.

FEEDBACK AND DISCUSSION:
Allow individuals to feedback on the experience if they wish to. How did it feel?

NOTE:
Ensure that the person's head is slightly tilted up to avoid dizziness.

(b) The Hammock
DIRECTIONS:

Ask the group to stand in two lines facing each other, with their hands crossed and clasping the hands of the person facing them, creating a hammock. A volunteer stands on a table edge, at one end of the line and when ready falls backwards into the hammock, keeping her/his body straight.

Offer this opportunity to each group member.

FEEDBACK AND DISCUSSION:
How did it feel? Are there other times in your life when you feel like this?

(c) Falling
DIRECTIONS:

Ask the group to move around in a section of the room. When someone chooses to, they call out loudly, 'oh no, I'm falling' and, pivoting from their feet, begin to fall backwards to the ground, keeping their body straight. It is the group's responsibility to surround and catch that person straight away. As the group become more confident you can spread out more around the room.

DEVELOPMENT:
No one calls out, they just begin to fall.

GENERAL NOTES:
These exercises are for older groups and should be played with a group who are very responsible, and have already developed a sense of trust.

5. Cat and Mouse II (see also Cooperation Games, Unit One)

Time:	10 minutes
Materials:	Shaker, blindfold

Number in Group: Minimum of 6

Aim: A group exercise to develop trust and emphasise
                          the need for group support.

DIRECTIONS:

Ask the group to stand in a circle. Two volunteers enter the circle and are
labelled cat (who is blindfolded) and mouse (who holds the shaker). The aim of
the game is for the blind cat to catch the sighted mouse, by touching them. The
mouse must shake the shaker when she/he moves. The group make sure the
blind cat is safe, maintaining an enclosed area. When the cat catches the mouse,
the round ends. Invite two new volunteers to take on these roles.

DEVELOPMENT:

The group can support either the cat or the mouse, by either increasing the size
of the circle (to help the mouse) or decreasing it (to help the cat).

FEEDBACK AND DISCUSSION:

How did it feel being the cat? The mouse? What is the importance of the
group?

Cooperation Games

A selection of games that allow the group to work together cooperatively with
a common aim, either as a whole group or in teams. This could be to support
each other in a common task, or solve a specific problem, enhancing trust and
continuing to build the group as a cohesive unit.

1. Grandmother's Keys

Time: 10–15 minutes

Materials: Set of jangly keys

Number in Group: Minimum of 5

Aim: Based on the children's game 'Grandmother's
                          Footsteps', this game gets the group working
                          together towards a common aim.

DIRECTIONS:

'Grandma' stands at one end of the room, turned away from the rest of the
group, and the set of keys are placed on the floor directly behind her at her feet.
The rest of the group try and get the keys back to where they start at the
opposite wall. They do this by advancing while her back is turned, but freezing
whenever she turns round. If she sees someone moving, they must go back to
the beginning.

Once the group have got the keys without Grandma guessing who is holding them, the keys must pass between at least four people's hands on their return journey. Grandma can have one guess at who is holding the keys, each time she turns round. If she guesses right, the keys are returned and the person holding the keys must go back to the beginning and advance again without being seen. The others then continue the attempt to steal the keys. If she guesses wrong, the game continues. Play two or three times with a different Grandma.

NOTE:

At first the group tend to try and grab the keys, without thinking through what to do next. As the group start working together, they will develop strategies for cooperation and succeed in getting and passing the keys.

2. Frogs and Alligators

Time:	20 minutes
Materials:	A drum or musical instrument that can be heard, newspapers
Number in Group:	Minimum of 4
Aim:	A fun game for developing support and physical contact among the group.

DIRECTIONS:

A 'pond' is set up through 'lily pads' of sheets of newspaper scattered round the space. The group are frogs, who perch on these lily pads, except for one person who is the alligator, and who stays in the pond.

When you play the drum, which indicates that the alligator is asleep, the frogs can move around the pond freely. However, when you stop, the alligator wakes up and tries to catch the frogs, who can only escape if they reach a lily pad, where they are safe. They cannot stay on lily pads while the alligator is asleep.

If they are caught, they become alligators as well, so the number of alligators increases all the time. More than one frog can shelter on a lily pad simultaneously.

At the end of each catching session, remove any free lily pads and tear bits off the ones that frogs are on, making them smaller and so harder to shelter on. Continue, until there is only one frog left – the winner!

NOTE:

The frogs need to cooperate and support each other, to save themselves and their fellow frogs.

3. Giants, Wizards, Elves

Time:	20 minutes at least
Number in Group:	Minimum of 6
Aim:	A team game fostering cooperation between participants, based on the principle of the children's game, 'Scissors, paper, stone'.

DIRECTIONS:

The group divide into two teams, one at each end of the room. Each team confers, and decides which group role they will take on first: giants, wizards or elves, then lines up opposite the other team.

At a signal, each team takes three steps towards each other and then at another signal take on the group role they have chosen, all making the same appropriate posture and noise:

Giants: arms above head and growling

Wizards: arms outstretched, zapping

Elves: bending down, fingers by ears.

(Any gesture may be used, as long as the group agree it, and it is clear which character is portrayed.)

Each character 'beats' another character thus:

Giants beat Wizards (through brute strength)

Wizards beat elves (through magic)

Elves beat giants (like mice scare elephants!).

When one team's role wins, they try and catch members of the other team, who run for their base. If they are caught, they must join the other team.

If both teams do the same posture, for example, giants and giants, everyone returns, grumbling, back to their bases and confers again on a role. The game then starts again. Continue until one team has clearly won, or until exhaustion sets in!

4. Saints and Sinners

Time:	10 minutes
Number in Group:	Minimum of 4
Aim:	To use the imagination, provide a release and develop cooperative teamwork.

DIRECTIONS:

Get the group into two teams. Give one team the role of 'saint' and the other team the role of 'sinner'. Ask both teams a question and allow them a few minutes to prepare and rehearse the most appropriate answer and accompanying gestures, in the manner of their role.

For example, if your question was 'Is anyone sitting here?' the 'saint' team might answer 'Why, certainly not – I have placed a chair there especially for you. Please let me wipe it clean before you sit down and I would be most honoured if you'd use my back as a foot rest'.

The 'sinner' team might then answer 'How dare you ask if that seat is free, you idiot, that's my seat, just because I'm not sitting in it at the moment – but let me spit on it first, before you sit down' etc. The team members have to answer in unison. Repeat with different questions and then swap the teams' roles.

DEVELOPMENT:

Rather than using 'saints' and 'sinners' make the roles relate to a theme, such as 'drug dealer' and 'drug user', 'policeman' and 'criminal'. This could be the starting point of a session on stereotypes.

NOTE:

Encourage the group's answers to be as wild and extreme as they can imagine.

5. Who Started the Movement?

Time:	10 minutes
Number in Group:	Minimum of 4
Aim:	A 'code' game, involving the cooperation of the group towards a common end, while one member has to 'break the code'.

DIRECTIONS:

Gather the group in a circle and ask for a volunteer to leave the room. The others decide who will start the movement, such as moving the arms. This person begins moving and everyone else copies, trying to make the movements simultaneous, so that no one is obviously leading. The person outside re-enters, and tries to guess who is leading the movement.

FEEDBACK AND DISCUSSION:

In terms of cooperation, was it easy or hard to make the movements simultaneous as a group? How might this relate to working on stage?

What about the person outside the group? How did they feel? How might this relate to a theme, such as bullying?

NOTE:
Keep the movements slow and fluid.

GROUNDRULES

These are vital so that group members feel safe within the structure of the project and have clarity about what is expected of them. All of us are used to being told how to behave – school, parents, work, the law, all give us rules which we have to abide by or be reprimanded accordingly. Usually these rules are phrased in the negative, such as 'don't run in the corridors' rather than in the positive, such as 'be safe and careful when moving around the building'. Also, the making of such rules excludes young people as they are never in control of deciding these rules and are rarely consulted in the process.

The setting up of groundrules with your group is a fundamental way in which you can begin to redress this lack of control, handing over the power and responsibility of the decision-making process to your group, but providing a clear structure which enables them to use it productively.

Being actively involved in the making of the rules can result in the following for group members:

- insight into the difficulty of creating laws that suit everyone
- an increased investment in abiding by the rules
- a sense of control, responsibility and self-worth
- a sense of ownership
- a challenge to the assumption that rules are made only by those in authority to abuse power and are intrinsically 'bad'.

The Contract

Time:	One and a half hours
Materials:	Flipchart, marker pen
Aim:	To provide a structured approach which includes all group members in deciding how the group will function.

DIRECTIONS:
Gather the group seated, around a flipchart. Explain that together you are going to construct the framework within which you all wish to work for the time of the project/session.

Ask members to think about the following:

(1) How do they want to be treated and treat others in order to enjoy and learn a lot during the project?

(2) What things need to be in place for them to work well as a group?

Brainstorm the group's responses on a flipchart. Add any of your own that you want to. Ask if there are any overlapping themes or words? Circle these and decide on a word or phrase for each of these that sums them up. Write these down on the flipchart if the group is happy with them. Aim for five words or phrases to work with. Now you need to focus these down into more specific points, for example, time-keeping could be focused down to 'I agree to be on time for all sessions and to phone if I know I will be late'.

Once you have achieved this, it is necessary to decide what will happen if the groundrules are broken. How does the group want to approach this? It is helpful at this stage if you raise some options with them, for example that you talk with the infringer alone about why they cannot abide by this particular rule; the infringer is asked to acknowledge their mistake and apologise to the group/individual concerned; the infringer is warned not to break the groundrules again; a group decision is made as to whether the infringer can stay with the group for the session/project etc. This is an opportunity for someone to change their behaviour and can be a positive learning point if handled sensitively.

At this stage it may be hard for the group to decide on a process when it is so theoretical; however, it is vital that they have some idea what happens if the guidelines are broken before an incident actually happens, rather than creating a process as it happens.

Once you have created both the groundrules and the guidelines for if they are broken ask the group members three questions to think about individually:

1. How does the contract support you?

2. How does it restrict you?

3. Which groundrule will you find most challenging?

The final stage is for everyone to sign the contract. This ritualistic act is important to symbolise group members' acceptance of the rules created.

VARIATIONS:
If you are only working for one day or session, it will not be appropriate to spend this amount of time on the contract. Perhaps you could create a few guidelines in advance, such as listening to each other's opinions and respecting each other's differences, and go through it with the group at the start of the session, asking them to agree to these for the duration of the session.

Figure 1.5 Participants create their own group agreement

FEEDBACK AND DISCUSSION:

The process of setting the groundrules is in itself difficult, especially at the start of a project when group members do not know each other. It is worth affirming the group's success at accomplishing this and reflecting on the process. Share in pairs: what was the process like for you? Why do you think we did it as a group?

A 'light and lively' may well be an essential after this!

If you are working together over a period of weeks or months you may wish to reflect halfway through the project on how the groundrules are being adhered to. Share in pairs: which groundrule do you feel has been infringed on most? Which groundrule have you broken and what happened? Are there any changes you think need to be made to the groundrules? Bring the group together as a whole to make any changes.

NOTES:

The groundrules need to be established early on in the project/course but after having allowed the group some time to relax with each other. Holding an introductory games/getting to know you session first is a good idea.

Setting the groundrules offers the facilitator the opportunity to suggest some essential 'rules' and to get the group to own them, such as no racist/sexist/homophobic language or behaviour.

Other subjects you may wish to raise if they are not mentioned are confidentiality; punctuality and non-violence.

Always refer back to the group so that ultimately they are making the decisions not you.

Stress that the contract is not carved in stone and it is for the group to question it and add things to it as the need arises. Keep the contract visible all the time while the group is working together so that you and they can refer to it.

Use of the word 'rules' may not be appropriate with your group. If you feel they will immediately resist this term, call it a 'framework', 'contract' or 'guidelines'.

Asking Someone to Leave

It might seem harsh to ask a group member to leave the group, but if one person is repeatedly breaking the groundrules and abusing the trust/safety of other group members it may be the only solution. This situation, if it arises, needs to be managed sensitively and yet firmly. Whilst group members are making a decision, make sure that it does not degenerate into a session of 'badmouthing' the individual concerned, but addresses their breaking of the groundrule and the alternative courses of action. Remember that it is the behaviour that is unacceptable and not the individual. Your responsibility is to the group *and* to the individual. If you are working with a colleague, it might be wise for one of you to talk with the individual and the other of you to facilitate the group discussion. If the decision is to ask the group member to leave, think about whether you or the group should tell them. Should they be given the space to voice their feelings to the group? Also, offer the individual some support once they have left – maybe to meet with you the following week and discuss their plans and thoughts with you. Try to make it as painless for them as possible, although it is obviously not going to be easy.

Once the individual has left, there may still be a need for reparations, as the group experiences guilt, discomfort and mixed feelings about the event. They may also be angry at you, feeling you have let them down. Make sure you plan time aside to voice these concerns and complement it with some extra group work, affirmation, fun games etc. Assure the group that this will be a great learning point for them, although they may not feel it now. Understand that it is painful and the group will need time to readjust. Do not blame yourself! Recognise that you too may need extra support and guidance around this event and seek it out where possible.

GROUP WORK

Often in mainstream theatre, or at work, or in training situations, a group of people are expected to work together with no particular framework for bringing that group together. When people are coming from different backgrounds, it is important to build on the foundations of the groundrules, by supplementing the drama work with exercises that bond the group. These exercises will let people feel safe enough to share experiences, and encourage personal and group responsibility for the information shared. The emotional trust involved in these exercises complements the physical trust of the games outlined above, and the exercises operate as preventative measures, rather than crisis responses.

The exercises also serve as an important way of exploring the issues further as a group, in pairs or individually, and developing personal and social skills, such as communication, listening and cooperation. The sharing of experiences further deepens the bond within the group and their investment in the project. For example, if looking at issues around drugs, it is important for the group and you to know the varying levels of knowledge and experience within the group. These can be gauged through, for example, brainstorming and personal stories about drug use. These stories also contribute to the core knowledge available to the group, and can then be drawn on in the devising process to reflect the participants' experiences in the theatre piece. Ritual is a useful tool in this work, for example the routine of the daily check-in (*see* Daily and Weekly Feedback, Unit One), providing a safe and understood structure for all concerned.

Exercises for Working with the Whole Group

1. Games (see Games, Unit One)

2. Brainstorming

Time:	2 minutes
Materials:	Large sheet of paper, marker pens
Aim:	A very useful exercise as a starting point and way into the issue; finding the level of knowledge with the group; finding associations around an issue which were not initially thought of; sharing information as a whole group.

DIRECTIONS:

Select the topic or word to be brainstormed, for example, homelessness, drama techniques, politics etc.

One person acts as scribe, and, within a time limit of two or three minutes, the group calls out everything they can think of associated with that topic or word. Nothing is censored and everything is written down.

DEVELOPMENT:

This can be used as a way into drama, using words as starting points for images, or scenes, or for further discussion. The group can divide into smaller groups, and then feed their brainstorms back to the bigger group.

3. Gatherings (see also Go Rounds, Unit One)

Time:	15–20 minutes
Materials:	None
Aim:	An exercise that gathers the group together and enhances trust within the group through the sharing of personal information. It also helps focus the group in preparation for a session of work, relating the theme to the session.

DIRECTIONS:

The facilitator offers a theme for everyone to respond to, and uses the go-round structure for the answers.

Figure 1.6 Brainstorming

EXAMPLES OF THEMES:

- One thing you'd like to do before the end of the year/millennium, and why
- Your favourite place to be, and why
- One person you admire, and why
- A pigeonhole or category that people put you in that you don't like, and why.

And so on.

NOTES:

Again, it is imperative that this space is not interrupted or commented on. People can have a tendency to ramble in this exercise, so encourage them at the beginning to be concise!

4. Hopes and Fears (see also Individual Work, Unit One)

Time:	30 minutes
Materials:	Scissors, coloured paper, glue, pens
Aim:	At the beginning of their work, this encourages people to think about their hopes and fears for the project. Together they discover shared experiences, and this therefore builds trust within the group.

DIRECTIONS:

Cut out balloon and kite shapes of coloured paper. Each person takes one of each shape and individually writes their hopes about the project on the kite shape, and fears on the balloon shape. Each person places their kite and balloon in a pile in the middle, face down, and when everyone has finished the pile is shuffled. Everyone then takes a turn to read one out anonymously, alternating hopes and fears. The kites and balloons are then stuck on to two sheets of paper.

FEEDBACK AND DISCUSSION:

Ask what the exercise was like to take part in. What were the similarities and/or differences between group members' hopes and fears?

NOTE:

If the two sheets are kept, they can be looked at again at the end of the project, as part of the evaluation process.

5. Paper not Floor

Time:	10 minutes
Materials:	Large sheet of paper

| Aim: | Group working cooperatively together, problem solving. Bonding the group. |

DIRECTIONS:

Give the group a sheet of paper. Their task is for *all* group members to be in touch with the paper but not with the floor at the same time. They are not allowed to stand on any objects, such as chairs. Initially, they will stand together on the paper on the floor; congratulate them but then reduce the size of the paper, a couple of times if necessary, until this is no longer possible. The way for them to solve the problem is to think laterally: they all hold on to the paper and jump in the air.

NOTE:

Give clues if necessary – the aim is for them to solve the problem together, successfully!

6. Daily and Weekly Feedback (see also Closings, Unit One and Evaluations, Unit Five)

| Aim: | Using the structure of a go-round, to give each other the opportunity to feedback on the day or week's work, or to check in at the beginning of the day. It is a space to speak, and a chance to gauge the mood of the group. |

(a) Daily Feedback: One Word Check-In

| Time: | 5 minutes |
| Materials: | None |

DIRECTIONS:

At the beginning of each day, in a circle, each person says one word, phrase or sound about how they are feeling that morning.

NOTE:

Encourage people to be sensitive to each other, if people are feeling low, but also to try and clear their mind and prepare for the day's work. A good routine to get into.

(b) Weekly Feedback

| Time: | 20–30 minutes |
| Materials: | None |

DIRECTIONS:

The group reflects on the week's work, using the go-round structure, again allowing uninterrupted space for comments, feelings, thoughts, experiences, problems, concerns and insights.

NOTE:

As above, the space is a non-judgemental one, and people cannot be interrupted, or comment on what has been said. You might find it helpful to introduce the idea of a 'speaking stick' which facilitates one person speaking at a time. A bowl of sweets can act as a speaking stick, and also act as a 'reward'.

Exercises for Working in Pairs
1. Personal Stories (see Individual Work, Unit One)

2. Three Ways of Listening (see also Individual Work, Unit One)

Time:	15 minutes
Aim:	To examine the process of listening, and explore how closely we really listen.

DIRECTIONS:

In pairs, each person has three minutes each. Person A talks about something they really enjoy, while person B listens. Give the instruction that:

(a) for the first minute, B is actively listening

(b) for the second minute, B is half listening

(c) for the third minute, B is not listening.

Swap over.

FEEDBACK AND DISCUSSION:

Feedback initially in pairs: how did it feel to actively listen? Was it easy? What body language did you use? How often do we actively listen? What body language did you use when half listening, or not listening? What about the person speaking – how did it feel with each level of listening? Did it change the way you told your story?

Now feedback to the whole group.

VARIATIONS:

Practise active listening in pairs, where each person has two minutes each to speak, and the other person cannot interrupt, even if it is to say, 'That happened to me!' When each person has spoken, give them another minute each to feedback to each other on what they have heard.

Another variation is each person telling how they got to the centre that day, for two minutes. Their partner then retells the story in the second person, 'You got up at eight' etc. Swap over.

Feedback questions include: how difficult did you find it to remember information? How does this relate to everyday life?

3. What's On Top of Your Pile?

Time:	10 minutes
Aim:	An active listening exercise which allows people to clear their minds and prepare to start work at the beginning of the week or session.

DIRECTIONS:

In pairs, each person has two to three minutes (timed) to tell the other person one thing on their minds that might prevent them from concentrating fully.

They swap over.

Give the pairs one minute each to feedback on what they've heard. Ask people to put this all to one side and focus on the week ahead. There is no further feedback or discussion needed after this exercise.

4. Mirrors

Time:	10 minutes
Aim:	A paired exercise using non-verbal communication, leading to trust and cooperation.

DIRECTIONS:

Get the group into pairs. Standing opposite each other, one person in each pair starts a slow movement, which the other mirrors – that is, as if looking in a mirror. The movements can gradually be built to be more complicated, but not faster. They swap over, without breaking the movement.

DEVELOPMENT:

Give the instruction that no one is actively to lead.

FEEDBACK AND DISCUSSION:

What did it feel like leading? Being led? Was it possible for no one actively to lead? What happened if this was successful? What happened if they didn't manage it?

Exercises for Individual Work

1. Personal Road Maps

Time:	30 minutes
Materials:	Paper, coloured crayons, pens etc.
Aim:	Individuals explore the process that has brought them to this point in their lives, identifying and acknowledging important choices, good and not so good.

DIRECTIONS:

Each person has a large sheet of paper and a selection of coloured crayons and pens. Each one draws a 'map' of their route to this point (for example home, school, work experience, college, important relationships etc.), marking the important moments and 'milestones' on the map.

The map is as individual as the person, and they can select as much or as little detail as they wish, but encourage them to try and deepen their reflection.

If the group wants, they can stick these maps on the wall as a 'gallery' – or they can just turn them over and keep them private.

DEVELOPMENT:

Get into pairs and talk each other through the maps and what they mean. Encourage active listening.

The important decision points on the maps could be used as starting points for the theatre piece.

FEEDBACK AND DISCUSSION:

If not already undertaken in pairs, people can choose to feedback on the exercise, either informally or as a go-round. What did the exercise bring up? How has their route through life brought them to this point? Has anything come up they hadn't thought of before? What information do we base our decisions on?

2. Personal Storytelling

Time:	Various
Aim:	For each member of the group to share personal experiences with the rest of the group, taking responsibility for the information they share.

DIRECTIONS:

Although the work is individual, it can be undertaken in pairs or small groups when participants are asked to share personal stories on a theme. If people do

Figure 1.7 Sharing Personal Stories

not have direct personal experience of an issue, then they may share stories about family members or friends, or even a news story that resonated for them.

Starting points might include: your first contact with drugs; leaving home or the place where you grew up.

DEVELOPMENT:

Individual experience can also be recounted in written form, such as diaries or letters, or in art work. These can be linked to drama work, so that personal experience can inform a character's 'diary' for example, offering a safe way to reflect group members' experiences.

NOTES:

Ensure that everyone understands that they are responsible for what information they share, and refer back to the groundrules on confidentiality. Also be aware that this can bring up some upsetting memories, but this might be a cathartic experience if freely undertaken within a supportive environment.

3. Where Do You Stand?

Time:	10 minutes
Aim:	To raise contentious issues with the group and encourage young people to develop their own viewpoint and listen to others non-judgementally.

DIRECTIONS:

Decide on a number of difficult statements to pose to the group, such as, 'Legalise drugs' or 'Capital punishment should be reintroduced'. Create an imaginary line running diagonally across the room. Explain that to stand at one end means you agree with the statement and to stand at the other end means you disagree, and that standing somewhere along the line means you agree/disagree to varying degrees. Make the statement and then call out 'go' for group members to run to the point on the line which reflects their opinion. Quickly ask for sentences from random participants to explain their position. Repeat with another statement.

DEVELOPMENTS:

This is a good starting point to explore difficult issues with the group. It can lead into a deeper debate on some of the statements, providing you create a safe structure to manage the conflicting opinions, for example, allocate roles for the young people to take on so they are one stage removed from the opinions voiced, regardless of their actual feelings on the subject.

NOTES:

Keep the exercise moving fast so that it does not degenerate into an argument. Do not allow people to respond to each other, except in the development of the exercise. Emphasise the importance of respecting the different opinions voiced, especially when they are different to your's.

CLOSINGS

Coming to the end of a session or day you may wish to bring the group members out of the activity they are immersed in and foster a sense of whole group unity. You may have identified the need to relax, to promote a sense of fun, a sense of exhilaration, a sense of achievement or to create a space to share reflections or voice anxieties.

The following selection of closings create a structured approach to your work, deepening the safety of the space and concluding the session in a responsible way.

1. Tropical Rainstorm

Time:	5 minutes
Number in Group:	Minimum of 5
Aim:	To bring down the energy level of the group, creating a sense of calm and cohesion.

DIRECTIONS:

Everyone stands in a circle: Go through with them the following different actions which make sounds:

- rubbing hands together
- clicking fingers
- slapping thighs
- stamping feet.

Ask the group to close their eyes and to repeat the sound they hear once the person directly on their left starts making it and to continue this sound until it changes to a new sound. You begin with the first sound which is made rubbing your hands together. Watch it build round the room until everyone is doing it, then change to clicking your fingers, then slapping your thighs, then stamping your feet. Now reverse the sounds to slapping thighs, clicking fingers, rubbing hands together and finally silence, each time waiting till everyone has adopted the sound before you change to the next one.

NOTES:

When this works it creates a wonderful effect of the building and calming of a storm.

You may need to keep an eye out, in case someone doesn't catch on to the sound and you need to help them.

2. Rainstorm Massage

Time:	5 minutes
Number in Group:	Minimum of 6
Aim:	To unite and relax the group, offering mutual support.

DIRECTIONS:

Gather the group in a circle, each person standing facing the person in front with her/his hands on their shoulders. Guide the group through a back and shoulders massage, which everyone gives the person in front of them at the same time, with the following.

The sun is shining warmly at the end of the day (long strokes) but gradually little drops of rain begin to fall (fingertips) as the sun goes behind the clouds. The drops of rain get heavier and heavier (harder pattering) and then out of nowhere the thunder starts to roar (whole hands) and the lightning strikes (side of the hands) and the wind howls (large circular motion). Slowly, the rain dies down (back to fingertips) and then the beautiful sun comes out from behind the clouds and warms everything again (long strokes).

NOTES:

Make sure people aren't too rough with each other. If there aren't enough people to make a circle, get people into pairs, who then swap over.

3. Pass the Pulse

Time:	5 minutes
Number in Group:	Minimum of 6
Aim:	To focus, unite and relax the group.

DIRECTIONS:

Sitting in a circle, the group holds hands and closes their eyes. Tell the group that when their right hand is squeezed, they must squeeze their left. You start the game by squeezing your left hand which passes a pulse right around the circle. Try to make the pulse pass round as fast as possible.

DEVELOPMENTS:

Introduce a second pulse in the opposite direction at the same time.

NOTE:

When this is working well, it will amaze the group how fast they can make the pulse circle the group.

4. Get Knotted

Time:	5 minutes
Number in Group:	Minimum of 6
Aim:	To provide a sense of achieving the impossible and working together as a team.

DIRECTIONS:

Ask the group to huddle together in a small circle, close their eyes and hold both their arms up in front of them, hands open. When they are all ready, they must find two hands that are free (preferably not both owned by the same person) and join their hands with them. When everyone opens their eyes, they must try to unravel the knot without breaking their hands.

NOTE:

This is usually very successful, but occasionally two smaller circles will be formed, or one part will remain knotted.

5. Count One to Twenty

Time:	5 minutes
Number in Group:	Minimum of 4
Aim:	To focus the group and provide a sense of whole group achievement.

DIRECTIONS:

The group sit in a circle with their eyes closed. The aim of the game is for the whole group to count out loud from 1–20, with people randomly calling out the next number. If two people say a number at the same time then the group must start again from one.

NOTE:

If 20 is too hard, try counting to 10!

6. Circle Sitting

Time:	5 minutes
Number in Group:	Minimum of 8
Aim:	To provide a sense of achievement and group unity.

DIRECTIONS:

The group stand in a circle, facing one direction and then move in, making the circle smaller until they are very close to each other. On the count of three, everyone sits back on the knees of the person behind. On the next count of three, everyone starts to walk, same leg first. This can be achieved in this position if everyone's weight is fairly evenly supported in the circle.

7. Texan Yell

Time:	5 minutes
Number in Group:	Minimum of 3
Aim:	To provide a sense of unity and exhilaration.

DIRECTIONS:

The group crouch down in a circle holding hands. Starting with a low hum, they gradually rise up, getting louder, until they jump in the air and yell loudly!

8. Make 'em Laugh

Time:	5–10 minutes
Number in Group:	Minimum of 5

| Aim: | To have fun as a group (and to practise not laughing when on stage). |

DIRECTIONS:

The group forms two lines, facing each other. One by one members of the group walk between the two lines, trying not to laugh, whilst the people in the lines make faces etc. to get the person to laugh before they reach the end of the lines.

NOTE:

No physical contact, such as tickling, is allowed.

9. Affirmation Pyramid

Time:	5 minutes
Number in Group:	Minimum of 4
Aim:	To affirm the qualities each member values in the group.

DIRECTIONS:

The group stands in a circle: Ask each group member to think of one thing about the group that they enjoy, respect or value, for example, the support offered by the group. One by one, each person places their hand (palm down) in the centre of the circle, on top of the hand before and say the one thing they thought of, until there is a pyramid of hands in the centre. After the count of three, everyone releases their hands in the air and remembers one thing that was said that they will take home with them.

NOTE:

Make sure people do not rest their hand's weight on the pyramid of hands, as the first person's hand will give way under the strain!

10. Go-Rounds (see also Group Work, Unit One)

Time:	10 minutes
Number in Group:	Minimum of 2
Aim:	To share a thought or feeling about the session and to voice concerns in a structured way.

DIRECTIONS:

Gather the group together, sitting in a circle. Give the group a theme and (if you wish) a structure in which to respond to that theme, for example, one word on how you feel now; a sentence on the best/worst moment of the day; one thing you have learned today; one time when you were angry.

Go round the circle listening to people's responses.

NOTES:

Make it clear that this is not a discussion, but a sharing of thoughts which are not to be interrupted, or commented on either during the exercise or afterwards. The group will soon get used to this method of feedback and begin using it naturally, although you may have to be strict at first.

People have the right to pass, but encourage everyone to say something.

ACTION RESEARCH

As part of the process of involving all participants in the planning and development of a project, Leap encourages action research about the issue by group members. This not only informs and educates in various ways, but also, through shared core knowledge, increases the sense of ownership of the project by the group – they have done the legwork right from the start, and there are certain important things they have discovered they want to voice.

The action research can take a variety of forms:

1. *Personal Stories*: (*see* pp.72–3 for structure): Personal experiences feed the core knowledge of the group, and offer the person whose story it is the chance to have their experience reflected in the final piece, for example by feeding the stories of the characters.

2. *Videos*: Various information videos are available on different issues, for example Centrepoint has resources on homelessness (see Resources). Independent production companies can often help with copies of broadcast programmes, and those made by community groups and young people themselves have the added bonus of showing an achievable aim.

3. *Speakers*: Workers from voluntary and statutory organisations may be happy to come and talk to the group, and answer any questions the group may have, as part of their job. They may also have additional material, such as case studies and videos, and suggest certain issues they consider vital for exploration.

4. *Written Materials*: Books, pamphlets, newspapers, magazines. These can be held at the centre, or you can suggest reading material. At Leap, we offer a fact pack, again with the aim of shared core knowledge.

5. *Case Studies*: These may come from material in books, personal stories, or from speakers, and offer a real insight into the issues.

6. *Theatre Trips*: If you are making theatre, why not try and see some theatre? Take the group to a local community drama performance or to the cheap seats in a mainstream or fringe theatre. If the piece is issue based, this is an especially useful way to look at how to dramatise issues, and can be really inspiring for the group. Focus on aspects of the production, through feedback and evaluation methods.

Note: Reading and writing may alienate some people. Ensure that you bear this in mind and use a variety of methods that they feel comfortable with.

This concludes Unit One, the first steps or preparation stage of your theatre project. Now that you have decided on the project structure and theme, recruited a group, and created a safe atmosphere for you all to work in, you are ready to explore the issues further and begin the training. Remember to keep returning to this unit for exercises and suggestions for work with your group throughout your project.

UNIT TWO

TRAINING TO MAKE THE LEAP

Once the groundwork has been done and the first steps taken, we can continue to prepare ourselves properly for making *the leap*. Now we must train ourselves mentally, physically and spiritually to make ourselves strong and ready to confront the change that lies ahead.

Unit Two: Training

UNIT GUIDE

Introduction
Exploring the Theme
Physical and Vocal Warm-Ups
Theatre and Drama Techniques
Engendering Leadership: Training in Workshop Skills

INTRODUCTION

This unit offers you a range of techniques and exercises to carry out the training aspect of the course. It focuses on theatre and drama skills, which can be utilised to explore an issue, complementing the exercises in Unit One, offering your group a common toolbox to draw on once they start devising. You could spend a session on each theatre technique to build up the group's repertoire, or only use the ones which you feel are most appropriate for your group and relevant to the aims of your work.

Accompanying the theatre and drama techniques are exercises and developments focused on the issue, and workshop leadership training as well. Don't forget the vocal and physical warm-ups which can become a regular feature in your day!

EXPLORING THE THEME (see also ACTION RESEARCH, UNIT ONE)

The exploration of the theme which your group has decided to focus on must be an ongoing process throughout the sessions of the project. In this unit, the theme can be further understood by utilising the action research methods described in Unit One as well as through the development and practice of new skills and techniques described below.

An example of using an exercise for exploring the theme and then using the drama technique for developing it further is given below.

The Tree

Time:	30 minutes
Materials:	Flipchart paper, marker pens
Aim:	A structured brainstorming exercise to look at the causes and consequences of an issue (e.g. drug use, violence, youth homelessness) and share related stories, leading on to drama work.

DIRECTIONS:

Draw the outline of a tree trunk on two large sheets of flipchart paper and pin it on the wall. Explain to the group that the roots of the tree are the causes of the issue and that the branches are the consequences.

Give the group three to five minutes to brainstorm all the causes they can think of and write them up in the 'roots' area of the image.

Do the same for the consequences, writing these down in the 'branches' area.

Clarify that the causes and consequences can sometimes be the same thing, for example, poverty can be a cause of homelessness as well as a consequence.

When the image is complete ask group members, one by one, to identify one cause and link it to one consequence, sharing it with the group in a narrative form, for example, 'a teenager runs away from home because he is beaten up by his stepfather (the cause). He stays on a friend's floor but has to leave and ends up on the streets with no money. His mental health suffers as he becomes depressed and anxious (the consequence)'.

Draw a line linking the two on the image.

DEVELOPMENT:

Drama work which could follow:

1. Split into smaller groups and ask each group to identify a cause and consequence from the 'tree' brainstorm and to create a frozen picture for these two different stages. Share the images with the whole group (see also Image Work, Unit Two).

2. Split into smaller groups and ask each group to identify a cause and consequence to create a narrative for, and improvise the story (see also Improvisation, Unit Two).

NOTE:

This exercise creates a clear visual image for people to relate to, and serves to simplify a complex interrelationship between cause and effect.

PHYSICAL AND VOCAL WARM-UPS

In an ideal world, every drama session would begin with a physical and vocal warm-up. Professional actors keep in shape by trying to do some exercises every day, and it is certainly useful with an inexperienced group who will need more relaxation and energising exercises than experienced performers.

The benefits of both physical and vocal warm-ups are various: more flexibility in body and voice, improved speech tone and increased physical and vocal confidence, and this increased fitness will help prevent strain or injury during exercises or performances. It is important for people to become aware of their bodies and voices and how they work and their levels of endurance and tension, and to take responsibility for themselves, knowing when to push themselves and when to hold back. Obviously, it is imperative that if anyone feels pain or dizziness they stop immediately.

It is particularly important to have regular warm-ups when you are rehearsing a piece of theatre, to warm up the actors and to help them focus on what they are doing, and it is necessary before a performance.

The warm-ups do not need to take very long, perhaps 15–20 minutes every day. Alternatively, you could run a full session on warm-ups, offering people a selection of exercises which they can then choose from for individual warm-ups.

This is a selection of exercises which build from relaxation and focus to more active work, using a mixture of Alexander Technique, yoga and vocal exercises.

The basis of all physical and vocal work is breathing – how we breathe affects the way we stand and move, as well as the way we speak. Most of us do not use our lungs to their full capacity, and we all have potentially much stronger bodies and voices, with greater flexibility and stamina.

Again, in all the exercises, emphasise that if participants experience pain or dizziness, they must stop – part of the whole process is taking responsibility for themselves and their bodies.

1. Physical Warm-Up

(a) Breathing (see also Vocal Warm-Up, Unit Two)
DIRECTIONS:
Ask everyone to find a space large enough to work in comfortably, then to stand still with their feet directly below their hips (not too close together or too far apart), with their arms hanging loosely by their sides.

Ask them to imagine a string through the middle of the top of their heads, that is pulling them up, so that they start to stretch upwards, rather than being pulled down by gravity. Be careful that the head does not tilt up, but stays looking ahead.

Ask everyone to breathe in gently through the nose, and out through the mouth. Do this a couple of times, but beware of hyperventilation.

DEVELOPMENT:

This work can also take place lying on the floor. Make sure that the back is spread out flat and supported by the floor, by raising both knees, with the arms comfortably resting at the sides. The head can also be raised on a jumper or even on a couple of books. Carry out the breathing as described above. Ask people to imagine that their breath is a column of air, and to aim it gently at the ceiling.

NOTES:

During initial breathing exercises, people may start involuntarily yawning. This is a natural response to more air coming into the lungs, and is not an expression of boredom! Emphasise that body parts are not to be dropped back on the floor, but carefully laid back down.

(b) Shake Out
DIRECTIONS:

Shake out each part of the body in turn: each hand; both hands; each arm; both arms; each foot; each leg; shoulders; hips. Finish with the whole body, shaking the head as well.

DEVELOPMENT: (see also Trust Games, Unit One)

Again, this can take place lying down, carrying out the exercise as described above. A further development is in pairs, where each person shakes out their partner's body, by gently lifting a hand, arm, foot or leg, and moving it about in the socket, before carefully replacing it on the floor. Finish with the head, taking the weight of the head in the hands, and moving the head from side to side, and up and down. Remember – do not drop any body part on the floor.

When people get up from work on the floor, they should roll over on to one side, and then get up. This prevents dizziness.

(c) Warm Up Different Parts of the Body
DIRECTIONS:

Warm up each part of the body in turn, and vary the number of repetitions according to the experience and ability of the group.

- Arms: hold one arm outstretched above your head, then move in a circular motion across the body. Swap directions. Swap arms. Do both arms together, in both directions.

- Shoulders: rotate each shoulder in turn, forwards and backwards, then together, forwards and backwards. Encourage people to start with small movements that can gradually get bigger.

- Ribcage: this can be quite difficult at first, as people may not be able to isolate the exact position and movement of the ribcage. Place hands on hips, and try and move the ribcage only, first from side to side, then forwards and backwards. After a few repetitions, move the whole ribcage round in a circular movement. The movements do not need to be very big.

- Hips: bend the knees slightly, and put hands on hips. Now swing the hips to one side then the other, then from front to back (very Elvis!). After a few repetitions, swing the hips all the way round in a circle (even more Elvis!).

- Feet: standing on one leg, rotate the foot of the other leg in the air, just off the ground. Describe circles, first one way then the other, and then figures of eight. Swap feet.

- Knees: standing on one leg, rotate the part of the other leg below the knee, making circles in the air. Swap legs.

- Legs: balance on one foot, and swing the other leg in a small arc from back to front, so it brushes the floor as it sweeps through. Gradually increase the arc size. Swap legs. And/or – standing on one leg, use the other leg to describe figures of eight in the air, swinging from the hip joint. Swap legs.

- Head: standing with the feet directly under the hips, tilt the head gently forwards then backwards, then from one side to the other. After a few repetitions, make a slow circle with the head, being careful not to turn the head as it rolls. Make sure that the mouth stays slightly open, especially when tilting the head backwards, and be sure to keep the movements slow and to alternate direction.

- Alternatively, imagine that the head is balanced on some ball bearings at the top of the spine, and gently rotate it on these, making a smaller circle than above.

(d) Whole Body Warm-Up

These exercises come from the Alexander Technique and focus on the back. Our bodies are often full of tension, like an armour of defence, and the source of the tension often lies in the back. The Alexander Technique starts with loosening the back, linked to breathing, in order to begin the work of relaxing and energising the rest of the body. This section can also take place before warming up the separate parts of the body described above.

DIRECTIONS:

(i) Swing:

This exercise can be used at the beginning or the end of the warm-up, or in between other exercises to keep loosening up.

Stand with the feet directly under the hips with the arms hanging loosely by the sides. Letting the head lead the movement, swing gently round from the waist, to one side and the other, so that the arms swing freely, while the legs stay in the original position. Imagine you are swivelling round the central 'pole' of your spine. You will gradually find your back loosening, so that you can swing a little further round.

When you finish the swing, don't stop abruptly, but gradually let the movement come to a halt of its own accord, so that the arms might still swing a little, when the rest of the body has stopped moving.

(ii) Swivel:

Still imagining the spinal cord as a central column which everything swings around, stand with the feet together this time, and the arms held by your sides. Let the whole body, from the feet up, swivel round the back bone, so that only the head stays still, facing front. Again, start off gently, then gradually increase the swing as you feel your back loosening.

(iii) Aerobic-type warm-up:

Here are some examples of aerobic type exercises:

- Run on the spot, starting gently, then getting faster and faster. Start to slow down again, get slower then come to a stop. This is a very quick energiser.

- Skipping, jumping, hopping, running.

Ask people if they know any similar exercises that they can teach the group, bearing in mind the need to state any do's and don'ts for each exercise.

DEVELOPMENT:

In a circle, each person starts an exercise, which everyone copies for ten repetitions. Go round the circle.

Dancing can be a great way to start the day, so encourage people to bring in music they like dancing to.

2. Vocal Warm-Up

The following exercises can be done either lying down on the floor, as described above, or standing up, or first one and then the other. They are a way of focusing on the process of breathing, as much as an exercise in themselves, and develop awareness of how the body works.

(a) Breathing
DIRECTIONS:
The ribcage:

(i) First stand with feet under hips, and breathe in through the nose and out through the mouth. Place your hands on your ribcage, both in front and behind, and feel how it expands and contracts as you breathe. Now breathe in through the nose and feel the ribs opening out, then sigh out through the mouth, pushing all the air out. Wait until you feel a movement in the ribs, then breathe in again slowly, feeling the ribcage opening out again. Repeat two or three times.

(ii) Breathe in, hold a moment, then breathe out slowly, counting to ten in your head. Keep the throat open, so the breathing out is noiseless. If there is any sound, then the throat is constricted. Always wait until you feel the rib muscles needing to move before breathing in again. Gradually increase the count to 15, over a few sessions.

Now you are going to deepen your breathing by exercising the diaphragm, which is the sheet of muscle which lies between the chest and the abdomen. As breath is drawn in to the deepest part of the lungs, the diaphragm contracts and goes down. As it relaxes and comes up again, the air comes out.

The diaphragm:

(i) Put one hand on your stomach, and give a very small sigh out, like panting but without jerking. Repeat, and feel the air going in and out. Stop if you start feeling sick, or dizzy.

(ii) Repeat, this time giving a small sigh out on the sound 'er' with a slight 'h' in front of the sound, vocalising it.

Repeat with 'ah', making a slightly longer sound

'ay', again slightly longer

'i', longer again.

Try singing the sounds, which will make them longer, and then join them together, 'ah, ay, i', as one sound, but not so that you over-extend the breath.

(b) Vocalisation
DIRECTIONS:
Now you are moving on to making sounds, moving around and becoming aware of how the body acts as a natural resonator.

(i) Stand with the feet under the hips, relaxed, and imagining a string pulling you up through the top of the head.

Bring the lips together and hum: 'mmm'.

Gradually bring the sound out into a sung 'aaah', remembering how the sound was created in the previous exercise, with an open throat.

(ii) Start walking round the room, repeating 'mmm-aaa', and trying different notes. As you walk, test where the sound is resonating in your body by putting your hands on your forehead, nose, cheeks and chest and feeling the vibrations.

When several people are doing this exercise simultaneously, the sounds created can be very beautiful.

(iii) Try other vowels: 'mmm-ay'

       'mmm-ee'

       'mmm-i'

       'mmm-o'

       'mmm-oo'

(iv) Ask everyone to find a part of the wall and aim their sounds at different levels of volume, and experiment with how the sound reflects back at them. Try different heights on the wall. (This is good practice for theatre performances, exploring how sound works in different spaces.)

(c) *Exercising Different Parts of the Mouth*
DIRECTIONS:

(i) Tongue:

Practise saying tongued consonants with different vowel sounds:

- la la la la
- le le le le
- li li li li
- lo lo lo lo
- lu lu lu lu.

You could make up different combinations of these, playing with different rhythms, and then go on to using different consonants:

- tah tah tah tah
- dah dah dah dah

- nah nah nah nah.

You could make up short tongue-twisters using these, and say them as fast as possible:

- dede nene dede nene
- tete dede tete dede
- lele dede lele dede

etc.

There are also the well-known tongue twisters, for example:

- She sells sea shells on the sea shore
- Peter Piper picked a peck of pickled pepper.

(ii) Back of the mouth: these exercises are for the back of your mouth, again using different vowels with the relevant sounds. Play around with these sounds, practising and repeating them, and using different rhythms:

- kah kah kah kah
- keke keke keke keke
- ko ko ko ko

etc.

Do the same with:

- gah gah gah gah

(iii) Using the lips, alongside different vowel sounds:

- pah pah pah pah
- bah bah bah bah
- mah mah mah mah

Repeat the following consonants:

- v v v v
- b b b b
- z z z z
- p p p p
- th th th th

Again, you can build these into rhythmic repetitions.

(iv) The whole mouth: imagine you have a large piece of chewing gum in your mouth, and chew it very thoroughly, working out all the muscles in the mouth.

(v) The face: screw up the whole face, including the eyes and mouth, as tight as possible. Now relax, and stretch out the face, eyes and mouth as wide as they will go.

For further information, refer to the book list in Resources.

Now you are ready to start work!

THEATRE AND DRAMA TECHNIQUES

As we leave childhood behind, we often leave behind our freedom to play and our belief in our innate creativity; the world becomes full of 'I can't' and 'I'm no good'. It is important for your group to recapture the enjoyment of using their imagination and to express themselves creatively before they are able to challenge themselves artistically. This section provides opportunities for developing the group's potential and expanding their drama and theatre skills to find new and imaginative ways of saying what they want to say. The techniques outlined are a selection of theatre tools, which Leap has found to be particularly relevant to young people without prior experience and with little education or training. They are rooted in the understanding that they are accessible to all of us and need no prior training to be utilised. This does not negate their sophistication or appropriateness to a more skilled group. The training that results from them is crucial to the empowerment process, equipping the group with a theatrical language which has the power to communicate their message.

Role Work

Exploring issues through drama, especially with young people with little drama experience, means that people take on roles within the drama that will often be very close to their own lives, and their own experiences will almost certainly inform the stories they create. This means that the work will be more truthful, they will have a higher investment in it, and they will have the opportunity to see their experiences told on stage and have their voices heard. However, this also has disadvantages as the boundaries between fact and fiction may become blurred, causing confusion with the potential to cause emotional upsets. It is important to have strategies that will keep the distinction clear, especially when people are in danger of losing the distinction between themselves and the character. Although you won't need to use them every time you create a piece of drama, the following techniques will assist you in making the boundaries clear when you judge it to be appropriate.

Personal Information

Ensure that everyone understands that they are responsible for the personal information they volunteer, that they feel safe about sharing it, and are happy to see it acted out, changed and discussed when it moves on into being part of the drama or theatre.

Roling Techniques

Each person should actively take on their role, perhaps by having a label with their character name on, so that everyone is aware they are in role and not themselves. When taking part in an exercise or in the initial stages of devising, although their own experience may inform what they do, this ritual will protect them, giving them a distance between themselves and the character they are playing. This gives the rest of the group the distance to comment, discuss, criticise and develop the character's story, and ensures that what you are doing is still in the realms of drama and not dramatherapy.

Deroling Techniques

The ritual of deroling is as important a part of the process as the roling. Ask the person to take off their label, and place it on a wall or chair, that is, separate to them, and then shake the character off, shaking hands, arms and feet. Ask them if there is anything they would like to say to that character, any advice they would like to give them. Then welcome the person back to the group by name, and ask them something about their lives, such as how they travelled to the centre that day, to root them back in real life.

By emphasising that they were in role, and that now they are no longer, you will be able to keep the boundaries clear for them. These boundaries are worth bearing in mind at all times during the drama work and as the participants become more involved in the devising, so that you can remind them that it is still a role they are playing, and not themselves. (*see also* Hotseating, Unit Three.)

1. States of Tension (*see also* Physical Warm-Up, Improvisation, Unit Two, Character Work, Unit Three)

Time:	30 minutes for initial exercise
	90 minutes including development
Number in Group:	Minimum of 2

Aim: A whole group exercise, focusing on the physical
                              effects of different levels of tension on the body.

DIRECTIONS:

Ask people to walk around the room as they would do normally. Tell them to
freeze. Now ask them to move around again, but this time as if they are
completely relaxed, so relaxed that they might fall asleep at any moment. Their
movements should be slow and heavy, if indeed they can manage to move at all.
This is Tension State One.

Ask them to notice how they feel moving like this: how far can they move?
How do they feel in themselves? How do they feel about the other people in
the room? Can they make eye contact with anyone?

They don't need to feedback at this stage, but just be aware of the effects of
this level of tension.

Now repeat this, moving round the room, building gradually up through
the following states of tension and reflecting that state through speed and
movement. Once they are moving in the new tension state, ask them to make
eye contact with other people, or greet them, and note how difficult or easy it is
in different states.

- Tension State Two: it is a lovely sunny day, they have no worries,
  and are walking through a meadow of flowers, listening to the birds
  singing.

- Tension State Three: they have a sense of purpose, something
  specific to do, but with plenty of time to get there and do it. No
  particular worries.

- Tension State Four: they are late and anxious that they might miss
  their train, but they have to get there on time.

- Tension State Five: now they are very late and are about to miss that
  train; they are extremely anxious and stressed out.

- Tension State Six: sheer panic and hysteria, the train is pulling out of
  the station but they absolutely must get there on time.

After they have reached Stage Six, and everyone is running frantically round
the room, ask them to freeze and then return to Stage Two, to relax everyone
and calm them down. Then finish.

FEEDBACK AND DISCUSSION:

Ask them to feedback what they noticed at the different stages from One to Six.
What happened to their speed? How did their movements change according to
the levels of tension, for example, shallow breathing, clenched fists, hunched

shoulders? How did they relate to other people at different stages? Were they able to avoid bumping into others? Could they get eye contact or greet each other? Did situations come into their heads for particular states of tension? Did any particular state feel the most 'natural' – that is, the one they are most used to using? Which felt the most unnatural?

DEVELOPMENT:

This can be used when creating characters for a theatre piece, as part of building the physicality of a character. It can also be used as a starting point for drama, where scenes can be developed giving people different states of tension within the scene.

FOR EXAMPLE:

Divide up into groups of four or five. One group gives another group a situation, for example waiting in the queue at the post office, and each person a state of tension to play. They then improvise the scene. The other group can freeze them and allocate new state of tension numbers, and let them continue the same scene. Swap the groups over. Feedback on the exercise: how did different states of tension affect what was happening in the scene? What characters developed out of the tension states? Did they recognise themselves in any of the characters' behaviour?

NOTES:

Allow people to experiment with different levels. The exercise offers an insight into our own behaviour and how it affects our bodies, movements and our surroundings, as well as being a useful drama tool in creating or building characters.

2. Status (see also Improvisation, Unit Two, Character Work, Unit Three)

Time:	30–40 minutes for initial exercise
Number in Group:	Minimum of 4
Materials:	Numbered slips, according to the number of people in the group
Aim:	A drama-based game exploring the meaning of status, and how it affects the way we relate to each other.

DIRECTIONS:

Before undertaking any status work with a group, it is important to discuss and clarify the meaning of 'status', and make sure that people understand the difference between status in society, which may be linked to wealth, looks or type of job, and the different levels of status that people use in different situations.

Point out that someone may have high status within society, but play low status with other people, and vice versa. A lot of comedy is based on this imbalance, such as the bored (high status) servant, with an anxious (low status) boss.

Ask people for examples of low status behaviour, for example, not looking people directly in the eye or avoiding direct confrontations. What about high status behaviour?

Explain that you are now going to give them the opportunity to experience different levels of status, with the chance to feedback in more depth afterwards.

Remember: status does not equal class.

(a) Divide everyone into two groups. As they walk round the room, one group holds eye contact with other people, and one group breaks it. Do this for a few minutes, then stop and ask for feedback.

> Feedback:
> How did each group feel? Superior? Inferior? Powerful, or powerless? Did they feel comfortable or uncomfortable with the role they were given?

(b) Now ask everyone to take a numbered slip, and not to tell anyone else what is on it. This is their status number in the group for this exercise, where number one is the highest status. Now they must walk around the room, relating to each other according to the status they have been given. This means behaving according to their own status number, and working out what other people's numbers are and responding to them accordingly. A low status number, 12 for example, cannot possibly have eye contact with number 2, but they may develop a friendship with number 11 or 13, although still maintaining the nuances of status. After a few minutes, ask everyone to get into a line across the room from one downwards, in the order they think they should be. Now go along the line and ask everyone to say their number. How close are they?

> Feedback:
> Were they more or less right, or were some people completely wrong? How did people make the decision? What did they notice that made them think someone was particularly high or low status? Were they correct? How does body language and eye contact affect status? Often people continue to confuse status with class, and produce stereotyped 'upper' and 'lower' class behaviour. Remind them that status does not equal class. Point out that someone

playing very high status does not *need* to be rude to anyone or even issue orders – they will get someone to do that for them.

(c) Run the exercise again, giving everyone new numbers, and this time ask one person to act as an observer as they move around interacting in their new status roles.

After a few minutes, ask the observer to place everyone in a line across the room, in the order they think they have seen.

> Feedback:
> How close are they? Why did they make certain decisions? Did some people think they were playing low, but actually played high? How far did their own status roles intrude? Someone who usually plays low status will find it very hard to play high and vice versa. What different roles do they play in different situations with different people?

DEVELOPMENT:

This exercise can be developed as a drama exercise, for creating and building characters, and as a starting point for improvisation.

FOR EXAMPLE:

In twos and threes, ask people to act out short improvisations in front of the whole group. Give them a situation and a status number: for example, a person begging from a business person; one flatmate has been helping themselves to the other one's food; a teenager has to tell her parents that she's pregnant. Try swapping the status round.

FEEDBACK AND DISCUSSION:

Again, highlight the differences between the status people play and the status given by society or age: a mother can be low status compared to her high status-playing daughter, and a homeless person can play high status with a low status-playing policeman.

What status roles are given to them by society?

Would they like to play a different status role, either higher or lower? Why?

3. Community Build Role Play

Time:	One and a half hours
Materials:	A large sheet of plain paper, coloured pens, labels, chairs
Number in Group:	Minimum of 3

Aim: To explore different attitudes and prejudices in a
                                safe, structured and fun way.

DIRECTIONS:

Gather the group around a large sheet of paper in the middle of which you have
drawn a crossroads.

Explain that this is the main road of a community which they are going to
create together, drawing the different parts. You might want quickly to
brainstorm what makes up a community: a school, a hospital, a playground, a
factory, houses etc. Make sure the group watch what each other is doing, so
they do not replicate. When they have finished, ask them to name the
community and write this on the paper.

Now, ask each person to decide on a character for themselves who lives in
this community and give themselves a name, decide where they live, work etc.
Encourage people to use this as an opportunity to try out a role very different
from themselves in age, gender and attitude. One by one ask each person to
introduce their character to the rest of the group and write their name down on
a label and stick it on their chest. Ask each character questions to establish
information.

Once everyone has introduced themselves, share a statement with the
group, which depends on what issue you wish to explore.

Planning permission has been given to build … (e.g. a homeless hostel/a drug
rehabilitation unit/a young offenders institute/an HIV/Aids Clinic) in the
community. There will be an open meeting to air community members' views
and decide on a course of action to be taken, whether to accept or oppose the
new plans.

Set up a circle of chairs where the meeting will take place and everyone will
participate in role. Ask for a volunteer to chair the meeting (or delegate the role
to someone you feel will be suitable). Place a time limit of 30 minutes on the
meeting.

Support the chair, suggesting that the meeting starts with their summary of
the plans and a go-round of everyone's views at this stage. Be clear that a
decision has to be reached by the end of the meeting.

DEROLING:

It is important to derole the characters after this exercise, especially if the
meeting was argumentative. You may do this by asking each person in turn to
remove their label and state one thing that is different between them and their
character. Once everyone has done this, tell them to run around and change
seats before starting the feedback.

FEEDBACK AND DISCUSSION:

Did the community reach a decision? If so, what was it and was it unanimous? What different attitudes were expressed in the meeting? What feelings (e.g. fear, ignorance) were driving these attitudes? What did you learn from this exercise? How realistic did you feel it was? Were the characters stereotypes? What other factors (e.g. media, government) feed into our attitudes?

NOTE:

This exercise provides the group with a safe and fun way to explore prejudices. It also allows inexperienced 'actors' to try out a character without the focus being on them.

4. Improvisation

Improvisation is the art of creating a scene or dialogue without any preparation and without a script. It is one of the basic techniques on which the devising process will depend. Improvisation involves being spontaneous, original, energetic, imaginative and cooperative. As we grow up we are encouraged to censor what we say so that it is appropriate to the setting and does not offend anyone – we learn that it is better to be safe than to use our imaginations. The following games aim to reverse this 'life' training and to encourage your group to be spontaneously creative, to develop their imaginations and to let their subconscious speak. (For further reading on improvisation *see* Resources.)

Improvisation Games

Aim: A choice of games to develop the group's spontaneity, imagination and confidence in a safe and fun way.

(a) *Mime a Lie*

Time: 10 minutes

Number in Group: Minimum of 3

DIRECTIONS:

Ask the group to stand in a circle. A volunteer enters the circle and begins to mime an action which is easily recognisable by the group, such as brushing their teeth. The next person comes into the circle and asks the person miming 'What are you doing?' The person miming does not answer truthfully, but lies, saying a completely different action, for example 'Playing the piano', and then they exit the circle centre. The person now remaining has to start miming the lie, until a new person asks them 'What are you doing?' at which point they tell a new lie. Continue until everyone has had a go.

(b) Change the Action

Time: 10 minutes

Number in Group: Minimum of 3

DIRECTIONS:

Ask the group to stand in a circle. A volunteer enters the circle and begins to mime an action. The next person enters the circle and has to copy the action and then change the context of the mime, for example the action of climbing a ladder could be changed to someone doing aerobics. Continue until everyone has had a go.

(c) In the Manner of the Word

Time: 15 minutes

Number in Group: Minimum of 4

DIRECTIONS:

Ask a volunteer to leave the room. When they are gone, the rest of the group decides on an adverb such as happily, superstitiously etc. When they have decided they invite the volunteer back into the room who has to guess what the adverb is by asking members of the group to do an activity 'in the manner of the word'. Different size groups can be asked to act it out. The volunteer is allowed three guesses. When they have guessed (right or wrong) a new volunteer leaves the room and the group chooses a different adverb. Continue until appropriate to stop.

(d) Change the Object

Time: 10 minutes

Materials: Any object can be used

Number in Group: Minimum of 3

DIRECTIONS:

Ask the group to stand in a circle. Introduce an object, such as a chair, to the circle and ask people one by one to enter the circle and mime a use for the object which is different from its real use, for example as a typewriter or a piano or a shoe. Encourage people to be as imaginative as they can and not to censor their own ideas.

DEVELOPMENT:

You can focus the exercise by giving the object a status, for example it is valuable/dangerous etc.

Encourage people to express an emotion in their mime.

(e) Persuasion

> Time: 5 minutes
>
> Number in Group: Minimum of 2

DIRECTIONS:

Ask the group to get into pairs and label each other A and B.

(i) A is the parent, B is the child. B wants something from A, for example to borrow money, to be allowed out, to have a friend to stay over etc. B has two minutes to persuade A to say 'yes'.

(ii) A and B are friends. A wants B to break the rules in some way, for example to take drugs, to play truant etc. A has two minutes to persuade B to do it.

FEEDBACK AND DISCUSSION:

Ask for a show of hands: who was persuaded?

Ask those who show their hands: what tactics worked best? Ask those who weren't persuaded: why not?

DEVELOPMENT:

Do not decide on the roles they are to play. Label them A and B and get them to establish their own roles through the dialogue.

You could also link the exercise to a theme such as drug use.

(f) Magic Box .

> Time: 10 minutes
>
> Number in Group: Minimum of 2

DIRECTIONS:

Ask people to find a space on their own, sit down in it and close their eyes. Imagine that there is a box in front of them. What does it look like? Is it large? Small? What is it made out of? Keeping their eyes shut, ask them to follow the imaginary shape of the box with their hands. Now get them to open the box. Is there a lock? Do they need a key? How does the box open? What's inside the box? How do they feel? Do they have a connection with the object inside? If they want to, ask them to pick the object up in their hands and feel it. Is it heavy or light? Put the object back and close the box. Ask them to open their eyes.

FEEDBACK AND DISCUSSION:

Ask the group to find partners and to share with each other what their boxes looked like, what the object was, who, if anyone, it reminded them of etc.

NOTES:

Encourage the group to imagine the finest detail. Prompt this through asking specific questions about the box and object.

(g) Pick Up

> Time: 5 minutes
>
> Number in Group: Minimum of 3

DIRECTIONS:

Ask the group to stand in a circle. One by one, ask group members to stretch down and to pick up something imaginary from the floor, stating what it is as they pick it up. Go round the whole circle a few times.

FEEDBACK AND DISCUSSION:

Was it difficult to think of something? Did you censor yourself? If so, why?

DEVELOPMENT:

You can use what is picked up as a starting point for an improvisation and get either the whole group or one other person to respond to the object and develop a dialogue.

NOTE:

When you are introducing the game, encourage people to say whatever is the first thing they think of and to try not to censor themselves or to pre-plan what they will pick up. Reassure people that there is no judgement being placed on what they pick up and that if they go blank they can say 'nothing'. Be aware when you think people might have censored their answer and substituted something else. Ask them if that was the first thing they thought of. You might want to do this game as a two-minute warm-up each day and see how the group begins to play with it more each time.

(h) Impro-Tag

> Time: 15 minutes
>
> Number in Group: Minimum of 3

DIRECTIONS:

Create a small acting area and seat yourselves as an audience. Ask for two volunteers (label them A and B) and give them a situation to improvise, such as dentist and patient in a surgery, mother and child on the beach etc. The rules are that they improvise until A makes a reason to exit and B freezes, whereby a third person (C) enters and starts a new scene. B has to take on immediately the new setting made apparent by C. After a few minutes, B exits, C freezes and another person (D) enters with a new setting which C has to respond to. Continue.

NOTES:

Encourage the group to keep the improvisations short and fast. Make sure that a person enters *immediately* as the person before exits.

(i) Argument Down the Line

Time: 20 minutes

Number in Group: Minimum of 4

DIRECTIONS:

Ask the group to stand in two lines facing each other. Label one line A and the other line B. At one end of the line, A starts an argument with B by making an accusation, for example, 'How could you have done that after all we have been through together?' B responds accordingly, building on the storyline that has just been created. The argument between the A side and the B side now moves down the line. All those on the A side answer as if they are the same person, and all those on the B side answer as if they are the same person. Once the argument reaches the end of the line, you can either end it there, or continue it back up the line again.

NOTES:

Encourage the group to develop the narrative of the argument with each addition, creating the characters and their situation through each line.

You may need to play this game a few times for the group to get more creative.

Starting Points for Improvisation

Once the group gets used to improvising you can use a number of different starting points to develop a scene.

The following are a range of possibilities:

- situations, for example, trapped in an elevator, after a burglary

- characters, for example a policeman and a young person begging

- lines in a hat selected randomly, for example a line of dialogue which has to start the scene, and/or a line of dialogue which has to end the scene

- a proverb which has to be illustrated or said in the scene, for example 'it never rains but it pours', 'don't put all your eggs in one basket'

- objects which have to be used in a scene, for example a bus pass, a lottery ticket, a photograph

- objects as stimulus for the drama, for example a piece of jewellery, postcard, picture
- a newspaper caption to base the scene on
- setting objectives so that the characters have to achieve something in the improvisation
- a personal story which is retold by the group
- a fact or series of facts to be demonstrated
- the lyrics of a song/music

DEVELOPMENTS:

Adding different states of tension or status levels (*see* States of Tension, Status, Unit Two) can deepen the complexity of the improvisation and add to the theatricality of a scene.

5. Storytelling

If the group is to take ownership and responsibility for the devising of the play, they need to have an understanding of what makes a good story and the skills needed to construct one. Drawing on their experience of film, TV, books etc. is a good starting point for them to think about what the components of a good story are. Ask them about what they enjoy, don't enjoy, about the plot, the characters, how the story concludes etc. The following exercises are designed to deepen their analysis of what constitutes a story.

(a) One Word Story

Time:	15 minutes
Number in Group:	Minimum of 3
Aim:	To use the group's imagination and practise the joint telling of a story.

DIRECTIONS:

Ask the group to sit in a circle. Explain that as a group you will make up a story with each person adding one word. Depending on how large your group is, decide on how many times you will go round the circle before ending the story. Ask for a volunteer to start.

DEVELOPMENT:

There are a range of ways to build from this initial one-word exercise. These include:

(i) Each person adds a sentence.

(ii) Each person finds an object in the room such as keys, a bag or a chair. They have to include the object in their sentence of the story.

(iii) Each person takes a line from a hat which they have to incorporate into their sentence.

(iv) Alternately use the word 'fortunately' and 'unfortunately' so that each person starts their sentence with either word.

FEEDBACK AND DISCUSSION:

After each round, ask the group: what worked about the story and why? What didn't work and why? Highlight the need for cooperation and concentration, querying how they impact on continuity. Discuss the importance of a beginning, middle and end of a story, having a central character, and, of course, the need for an engaging storyline!

(b) Whose Story is it Anyway?

Time:	20 minutes
Number in Group:	Minimum of 6
Aim:	To examine the key elements of a story, drawing on personal experience.

DIRECTIONS:

Get the group into pairs and ask each pair to tell each other a story about a time when they were naughty as a child. Now ask each person to find a new partner and to tell them the story they were told by their last partner as if it happened to them. Continue this three or four times. Gather the group together in a large group and ask each person to tell the story they just heard in the last round of exchanges, as if it is their own.

FEEDBACK AND DISCUSSION:

Does each person recognise their own story? How have the stories changed? Why have the stories changed? What elements of the story have been lost? How does this inform our own devising process?

DEVELOPMENT:

Add a rule to the retelling of the story, for example to add an ending from a fearful perspective, a resolved perspective etc.

NOTE:

Make it clear that the stories people share will be heard by the whole group and encourage them not to use a story which is too personal.

(For other examples of personal storytelling *see also* Group Work, Unit One.)

(c) A Modern Day Fairy Tale (see also Improvisation, Unit Two)

    Time: 45 minutes

    Number in Group: Minimum of 6

    Aim: To develop storytelling and improvisation skills
                            whilst highlighting the importance of the audience.

DIRECTIONS:

As a group decide on a well-known fairy tale such as Snow White or Cinderella, and make sure everyone knows the basic storyline. Split into three smaller groups and set each group the task of reworking the story for a modern-day audience (20 minutes). Give one group an audience of children, one group a teenage audience and one group an adult audience. Share all three versions.

FEEDBACK AND DISCUSSION:

What considerations did you make when reworking the story? How did the three versions differ? What is the importance of targeting a particular audience? How will this inform our own devising process?

NOTES:

As the groups are working, go round to each group to offer help.

Also use fairy tales which are not Eurocentric, but are drawn from other cultures.

(d) Image Storytelling (see also Image Work, Unit Two)

(e) Bard's Chair (see also Improvisation, Unit Two)

    Time: 20 minutes

    Materials: A chair

    Number in Group: Minimum of 4

    Aim: To introduce the role of narrator, giving everyone
                            the opportunity to try it out.

DIRECTIONS:

Set a chair in the centre of the room. Ask for a volunteer to sit in the chair and start to make up a story whilst everyone else acts it out. When someone wants to take over as the bard (the storyteller), they tap the person in the chair on the shoulder and take over the seat, continuing the story where it was left off. The old bard rejoins the others acting the story out. Continue until everyone has been the bard.

FEEDBACK AND DISCUSSION:

What was it like being the bard? What was it like acting out the story? What role does the narrator play in a theatre piece? In what different ways could you tell the story?

NOTE:

Encourage those acting out the story to interact with each other and take on different characters in the story.

DEVELOPMENT:

Split into groups of three or four and ask each group to take a story they all know, for example from a film, and decide on the five main points in the story. Act the story out using a narrator. Explain that they need to make sure everyone takes on the narrator's role in the story and think about how they swap roles.

6. Voice and Sound

Making music doesn't always require the ability to play a musical instrument or to read music. It is possible to encourage and inspire young people to participate in music making despite initial reservations which arise from feeling unskilled. We can learn to recognise and value our own potential if the starting premise is one of possibility. The following exercises are examples of the numerous ways in which we can use sound, voice and rhythm to express our feelings, re-create the world around us, develop coordination and listening skills and communicate with and entertain others.

(a) Call and Echo

Time:	10 minutes
Number in Group:	Minimum of 3
Aim:	A simple exercise to develop our listening and rhythmic skills.

DIRECTIONS:

Ask the group to stand in a circle. Begin a pulse of four (stamp, click or clap it) and encourage everyone to join in. Ask for a volunteer to sing or chant a short phrase (with words or sounds) which the rest of the group then echoes. Continue round the circle, so that each person contributes a phrase.

DEVELOPMENT:

- Theme the round based on an issue, such as conflict.
- Add a movement to the sound.

FEEDBACK AND DISCUSSION:

Ask group members to feedback briefly on the exercise stating whether they enjoyed it or found it embarrassing, difficult etc. Use their feedback to measure their confidence and to inform the speed at which you progress through the exercises.

NOTE:

Encourage people to vary their sounds, trying different pitches and volumes on each round.

(b) Circle Music

Time:	One hour
Materials:	Various everyday objects, percussion instruments
Number in Group:	Minimum of 3
Aim:	To develop rhythmic skills and explore the potential of creating music from objects, instruments and our voices.

Figure 2.1 A drumming workshop

DIRECTIONS:

(i) Ask people to find an object from the room such as a pen, notepad, keys, etc. and to experiment on their own with how many different sounds they can make with that object. Gather the group together in a circle. Over a basic pulse, ask a volunteer to make a repeated sound with their object. One by one get everyone to join in, fitting in their object and sound, listening to each other. Bring to silence. Try again with different sounds from the same objects and then with different objects.

(ii) As with (i) but using sounds made with the body and voice – clapping, clicking, flicking etc.

(iii) As with (i) but using a variety of percussion instruments such as tambourine, drum, triangle, shaker.

(iv) As with (i) but using a sung phrase or word, based on a theme such as names of countries, types of fruit, homelessness etc. Add a movement too. Change your phrase still listening to how it fits in.

DEVELOPMENT:

Decide on a visual cue for getting louder, softer, stopping and starting and take on the role of conductor to experiment with different volumes, bringing one sound in louder than others, stopping half the group etc. Let group members act as the conductor. See if the group can change the volumes etc. without a conductor, by listening and responding to each other.

FEEDBACK AND DISCUSSION:

What worked well and why? What didn't work well and why? How did they communicate without a conductor? How might this be used in a theatre piece?

NOTE:

Encourage the group to 'play' with the sounds and instruments.

(c) *The Band*

Time:	20 minutes
Number in Group:	Minimum of 4
Aim:	To work cooperatively to create a musical band without instruments.

DIRECTIONS:

Divide into groups of four or five. Ask each group to experiment with re-creating the sounds of musical instruments with their voices, such as drums, trumpet etc.

Decide on which person is which instrument and who will be the conductor. Using visual cues, the conductor can bring in different instruments, stop the music, make it louder, quieter etc. Prepare an easy song for the other group. Share.

DEVELOPMENT:

Introduce actions as well as sounds for the orchestra. Try giving the orchestra an emotion to communicate or giving individual instruments emotions.

FEEDBACK AND DISCUSSION:

What worked well and why? What didn't work well and why? How might this be used in a theatre piece?

(d) Sound Pictures

Time:	15 minutes (45 minutes with development)
Materials:	Percussion instruments (not essential)
Number in Group:	Minimum of 3
Aim:	To communicate an idea, place, theme or emotion through sound.

DIRECTIONS:

Ask the group to sit in a circle and close their eyes. Give them a setting, such as a market-place, seaside or city, which they have to create as a group through sound effects made by their voices and/or bodies. Ask for a volunteer to start with a sound and, one by one, for the others to join in. Do this a number of times with different settings, emotions, themes and ideas.

DEVELOPMENT:

(i) Divide into groups of three or four. Give each group the name of a country which they have to re-create using sounds. Ask them to create a frozen picture to accompany the sound, adding a visual dimension. Share the prepared pieces for the others to guess.

(ii) Divide into groups of three or four. Give each group a series of three ideas which they have to re-create using sound (including instruments if you wish), moving smoothly from one to the next, for example, a storm, the morning, the street. Share the prepared pieces for the others to guess.

(iii) Ask for a volunteer to sit in the centre of the circle and state a place where they would like to be, for example a funfair, on holiday, in the countryside. They close their eyes and the rest of the group creates the place for that person through sound. Bring to a stop. Continue until everyone has had a go.

FEEDBACK AND DISCUSSION:

What worked well and why? What didn't work well and why? How might this be used in a theatre piece?

7. Machines

Time: 10 minutes (20 minutes with development)

Number in Group: Minimum of 3

Aim: To express ideas physically as a group.

DIRECTIONS:

Explain that you are going to create a moving machine, as a whole group. One person comes into the middle of the circle and starts a rhythmic movement that can be repeated, like a machine. A sound can also be added. Ask another person to come and add a new movement and sound, fitting in with the last one as if they are a different part of the same machine. Each person gradually adds their new moving part and sound, to create a whole machine.

Imagine that you can crank the machine up, and run it at different speeds, fast and slow, before bringing it to a stop. Allow people time to feedback informally.

DEVELOPMENT:

Now you can offer themes for people to create machines in smaller groups and use words/phrases as well as sounds, for example: an anger machine; a love machine; a youth machine; a Great Britain machine; Tory and Labour machines. In an anger machine the movements would be sharp and strong, perhaps with fists held up and the phrase might be 'I hate you'.

Figure 2.2 A media machine

The machine could be linked to the theme of the workshop, such as a homelessness machine, or a conflict machine. Newspaper captions could also be used as starting points. Allow the groups time to show their machines to each other.

Machines can be used as part of a theatre piece, perhaps as a choreographed piece of group movement, particularly when using sound as well (*see also* Devising a Theatre Piece, Unit Three).

FEEDBACK AND DISCUSSION:

This exercise can throw up some interesting interpretations of a word or idea. What new or different aspects did they discover within the machines?

NOTE:

This exercise is quite abstract, and requires patience with the repetitive movement and so may appeal more to older groups than younger ones.

8. Physical Theatre

Theatre has been hugely influenced in recent years by mime artists and physical theatre practitioners, illustrated by the rise of training schools, such as the Lecoq school in Paris, and Circus Space in London, whose work has filtered down into youth and community theatre. Physical theatre can be very useful when working with a group who find language difficult, and can be successfully mixed with text-based or scripted work to make interesting, visually dynamic theatre. In addition, it encourages participants to exercise and stretch their bodies, as well as creatively expressing ideas without language, and is a strong component of the 'poor theatre' concept, that is theatre without set or props, where location, object or mood can be shown by the actors' bodies; it can also be used as an effective contrast to naturalistic work.

There follows a series of exercises that can be explored separately, but can also be linked together to create a complete session on physical theatre, building to telling a story with few or no words.

NOTE:

Before beginning these exercises, you will need to lead a physical warm-up (*see* Physical Warm-Up, Unit Two).

(a) Isolating Movement/Body Awareness

> Time: 20 minutes
>
> Materials: Chairs
>
> Number in Group: Minimum of 2

Aim:	A basic mime exercise, encouraging people to be aware of movement in different parts of their bodies.

(i) In pairs, A walks to a chair and sits down on it, while B watches. B then feeds back on what unnecessary movements took place in the process – it is interesting to see how many extra movements we make, such as head or hand movements. Let A try a couple of times to sit down on the chair whilst only moving the parts of the body that really need to move. B can watch and coach them. Then swap over. This is a good starting exercise to get people to isolate their body movements.

(ii) Still in pairs, A imagines that their finger has an electric current at the end of it. They will use this to poke B (gently!) on different parts of her/his body, while B needs to try and isolate their response to the 'shock' to only the part that has been touched – just the finger or part of the arm or knee or whatever. Try different parts of the body, then swap over.

(iii) Still in pairs, stand a few feet apart. This time, B is like a puppet, with pieces of string attached to different parts of her/his body. A now moves the 'string' to raise, lower or move the different parts of B's body, arms, head, knees, feet etc. Practise a few times, really trying to isolate the movement, and removing any extraneous movements. Swap over.

DEVELOPMENT:

These exercises can be taken on to very basic mime technique. Working individually, each person combines the string movement with the jolt of the electric shock, for example: move one arm as if you are a puppet and your arm is on a string, but stop the movement with a very small spasm, before moving the arm on in a new direction and stopping again with a tiny spasm. This creates an almost 'robotic' effect, and is the start of mime work. Practise picking up imaginary objects, concentrating on precise, isolated movements that are carefully placed and carried out. At a later date, this work can be strung together to create more fluid movement, but these exercises are a good starting point in physical awareness and concentration.

(b) *Stylising Actions/Movement into Theatre*

Time:	20 minutes
Number in Group:	Minimum of 2
Aim:	To build on isolating body movements from the previous exercise, and transform everyday movements into stylised actions, as a basis for choreographed group work.

DIRECTIONS:

Individually, find a space to work in, and think of an everyday movement, such as a household task, for example washing windows or sweeping the floor. Ask everyone to mime their action, and then repeat the movements for this task.

They then reduce the number of actual moves within the larger movement to 10 or perhaps 12.

For example, if the action is washing the windows: the first move is the arm moving down to the bucket; the second move is the arm moving up with the sponge in hand; the third move is the first wipe across the window and so on. Combine these into one fluid movement, spending some time practising them until they have learnt the whole sequence, then show some to the whole group. Try combining the action sequences in twos and threes, and then in two groups so that the other group can watch.

Seen together, the actions become a sequence of choreographed movement.

DEVELOPMENT:

This work could be used in a theatre piece to show a location without words.

(c) Physicalising Objects

Time:	15 minutes
Number in Group:	Minimum of 2
Aim:	To practise representing objects with body shapes and movements.

DIRECTIONS: (see also Mill, Grab and Tab in Image Work, Unit Two)

Using this game structure, ask people to show objects such as: telephone, armchair, doors, typewriter, clock, wall. They can add sound, but not script. When the groups are showing their objects, see if you can 'use' them and see how they work, for example are the doors revolving or swing doors?

DEVELOPMENT:

This work can be used when creating a piece of theatre, and can be extremely effective, as well as entertaining for the audience.

(d) Physicalising Places

Time:	10 minutes
Number in Group:	Minimum of 2
Aim:	To use body shapes and movements to represent a place or location accurately enough for an audience to understand.

DIRECTIONS:

In small groups, select a location and show it to the rest of the group, without words, so that they can guess the place. This does not have to be frozen.

For example: a tennis match; a restaurant; behind teacher's back; a horror film at a cinema.

NOTE:

This exercise relies on the coordination and timing of the group, and they may find it easier to do it in slow motion at first.

(e) Essential Movement

> Time: 45 minutes
>
> Number in Group: Minimum of 3
>
> Aim: To tell a story in mime and gesture, in a timed exercise to ensure only the most essential movements are used.

DIRECTIONS:

Give everyone the same basic story to work from – for example, 'the dumb show' from *Hamlet*. This is the story in its most essential form. The king and queen are married. While the king is sleeping, the king's brother pours poison into his ear, killing him. The brother courts the queen, who then marries him.

(i) Get people into groups of three and ask them to show this story without words in a version taking one minute, using only their bodies to physicalise the action. They must include every element of the story and represent each character clearly.

Give them ten minutes to prepare and rehearse, reminding them to think of the essential elements of the story.

They then show their versions to the rest of the group and are timed.

FEEDBACK AND DISCUSSION:

Most groups will go over the time limit, but encourage feedback from the audience on how they could hone it down, for example: cutting unnecessary exits and entrances, encouraging freezes instead; cutting any extraneous characters or story elements; using other ways of representing character or status.

(ii) Now ask people to do the same thing again – in 30 seconds

(iii) Now ask them to do it again – this time in 10 seconds!

The last approach ensures that each group is forced to remove any extraneous activity, and tell the story clearly. Each time, ask for feedback from the rest of the group, and concentrate on only the essential elements of the story.

(f) Physicalising Stories

Time: 45 minutes

Number in Group: Minimum of 2

The final piece of this work involves putting all of the previous elements together to tell a whole story without words, perhaps as part of the theatre piece.

DIRECTIONS:

This exercise asks people to use a well-known story, perhaps a fairy tale, and then to recap on all of the above methods to tell it physically.

At this stage, they may want to introduce some sound, but any words should be kept to the absolute minimum.

Share and feedback.

FEEDBACK AND DISCUSSION:

What worked effectively? Did the audience understand the story? How could it have been improved?

9. Image Work

The technique of images, also called frozen pictures, tableaux, still-images and freeze-frames, is one of the most versatile techniques available to you. It can be used by itself, exploring what is happening within the picture by, for example, asking people what they are feeling in the image; or it can be used as a way of developing scenes and characters, and so taken on into creating theatre. Young people find it easy to understand in television terms, as a freeze frame, and it is particularly useful for people with little or no experience of drama, as it feels safer than having to go the whole way and improvise a scene. The pictures can be closer to our true feelings than words might express, as the analytical side of our brains often censors these feelings whereas the physical nature of images offers a more immediate, even instinctive, response.

It is also a more democratic way of working with people who are less verbally articulate, and this was one of the elements that contributed to the Image and Forum Theatre structures developed by Augusto Boal. For further information on, and development of, Image and Forum Theatre, please refer to *Games for Actors and Non-Actors*, by Augusto Boal (*see* Resources).

The following exercises use images both as outcomes in themselves, and as a method of creating theatre.

Image-Based Games

Aim: For the participants to use their bodies to express ideas or situations, working individually and cooperatively.

(a) Mill, Grab and Tab (see also Ice Breakers, Unit One)

Time: 10 minutes

Number in Group: Minimum of 2

DIRECTIONS:

Ask the group to move ('mill') around the room. Then ask them to get into groups of two, three, four, or whatever ('grab'). In their groups, give them an idea, issue, object or location, which they have to express in a frozen picture or tableau ('tab'). Examples might be: the number six, the letter K, a football match, a party, parent and child, teacher and pupil, friendship, home, trust, conflict, etc.

Ask the groups to stay frozen, while you quickly move around checking and affirming their work, highlighting any aspects you can immediately see. Repeat four or five times, using different words and different sized groups, if you have enough participants.

NOTES:

The exercise can be used to split a large group into smaller groups, or to bring everyone back together as a large group. It is an excellent introduction to image-based work, but could also be used as an ice breaker for a new group.

You can also link the exercise to the theme of the workshop.

(b) What's the Story?

Time: 10 minutes

Number in Group: Minimum of 2

DIRECTIONS:

Demonstrate this exercise with a model: ask for two volunteers to step towards each other, shake hands and freeze. Ask the rest of the group to look at the picture created and think what the story is — two business people agreeing a deal? Graduation day? Then ask one person, A, to step out, removing half the picture, while the other person, B, stays frozen. What could a new story be now, of B standing with their hand held out? A priest blessing someone? A teacher demonstrating something? If someone suggests something, ask them (C) to step in and complete this new picture with a frozen gesture. Then ask B to step out. What might this new picture be – and so on.

Now get the group into pairs, and ask them to try doing the same thing, using their bodies to alternate freezing and completing the image. The image doesn't have to make immediate sense, so they can use their bodies abstractly to complete the picture.

FEEDBACK AND DISCUSSION:

Allow the pairs time to feedback to each other, and then ask for feedback from the whole group. Was the exercise difficult? If so, why? What made it easier?

DEVELOPMENT:

The exercise can be developed using three people, where two people freeze and the third steps out, then comes in to create a new picture; or a chair could be added, or a different object.

NOTES:

The important thing is to 'think with their bodies' – not their analytical heads – so encourage them to move quickly and not stand and look too long.

At first, people will try and be clever, which will stop them being spontaneous, but once they get into the rhythm of thinking with their bodies, it can be a very releasing experience.

(c) Circle Turn

Time: 15 minutes

Number in Group: Minimum of 2

DIRECTIONS:

Ask everyone to stand in a circle facing outwards, that is, away from each other, so that they will not be influenced by others' ideas.

Call out a word, which can be an emotion or idea, and then count to three. On 'three', they turn back into the circle and make a frozen image or picture of that word, using their bodies. Examples of words you might use include: fear, anger, youth, joy, teacher, politics, hope, home, woman, man etc.

Repeat several times, using different words, encouraging people to think about the different levels available to them.

Ask them, while frozen, to look round the circle to observe what other people are doing.

FEEDBACK AND DISCUSSION:

What similarities were there among the images? Did any images surprise or shock them? Did they find it easy to make the images? Did they find themselves reproducing what other people were doing?

DEVELOPMENT:

After these individual images have been created, start linking them up. Ask people to look at what others are doing, and if they think they form a 'family' of images, to move towards them and freeze again in their group image. Or do it in twos, where people move towards a complementary image.

These pictures can then be brought to life and explored (*see below* Bringing the Images to Life) or they can be used as starting points for scenes or to create characters. What is happening in this image? Who are the characters in it? People do not need to stick to their original thoughts and ideas, but can develop them to create new stories.

The images can be linked to the theme of the workshop.

NOTES:

Sometimes the images created are stereotypes, an understandable quick response to the stimulus. It can be very interesting to go back to certain words, when the group are more comfortable with the work, and ask people to form images again, as these later images are often very revealing. Ask for feedback on how and why the images changed.

(d) Group Images

There are several ways of developing a group image. Here we have described the method we use the most, which is probably the simplest.

Time: 20–30 minutes

Number in Group: Minimum of 4

DIRECTIONS:

As a whole group, brainstorm the issue or word that you want to explore. In smaller groups, of fours or fives, each group selects one of the words from the brainstorm and, as a group, creates a frozen picture of that word, that expresses their feelings about it.

This can be an abstract expression of the word, or, if you want to use the image as a starting point for drama, ask each group to embody a conflict of some kind in the image.

FEEDBACK AND DISCUSSION:

Ask each group to show their images to the rest of the group, then ask the audience to feedback on what they see. Explain that this is an important part of developing the work as theatre – how an audience interprets the arrangement of bodies in an empty space might be quite different to what the group have intended, but equally valid. The group should remain frozen and listen to this feedback, before they respond, so that they hear all the interpretations, which may offer insights they hadn't thought of and feed their story further, and so that they don't influence the audience's response. This is also an important part of the process of investing personal information and responses into the work, which then go on to be reworked into the theatre piece, and 'letting go' of these personal stories.

Ask the audience: if the image is abstract, what are they representing? If it is naturalistic, what is the story? Who is the central character? What is the conflict?

Once the audience has fed back, offer each member of the performing group the chance to feedback.

Bringing the Images to Life

Here we provide a list of possible ways of bringing the images to life, in order to explore further the thoughts and feelings of the characters within the picture, what their relationships are, and the tensions and conflicts embodied in the image. They can be used with Circle Turn and with Group Images (*see* Unit Two) and should be read in conjunction with both the exercises themselves, and the development section. They can be used separately, or combined.

- TOUCH AND TELL: with the actors still frozen in the image, touch each actor on the shoulder and ask them to say one word that describes how *their character* is thinking or feeling in the image. This not only informs the actor playing that character, but also the other actors in the image.

- ADD A MOVEMENT: each character makes one movement, *as their character*, which they repeat like a machine. This movement should be indicated by the image – for example, if someone has their hand outstretched, their repeated movement might be to try and shake someone's hand.

- ADD A MOVEMENT AND WORD/SOUND: combining the two techniques, they add one word or sound, and one movement.

- INNER MONOLOGUE: using Touch and Tell, each character has up to three minutes to say everything they are thinking and feeling as the character, in the form of a monologue. Encourage them to use the whole time, as they will start to dig deeper and further feed the characters and story. Their impressions of the story will be adapting continuously, but they are developing the story as a group. This section can be informed by the word and movement work above.

- SLOW MOTION: within the image, each character now moves in slow motion to where they want to be – with someone else, away from the action, or whatever. Of course, the other characters will also be moving and may have different ideas. Freeze after a few seconds, and feedback on the changes that have happened.

- MOVING TO THE IDEAL: if the initial image is one of oppression of some kind, such as unemployment, racism or homelessness, ask the group to move in slow motion to their ideal picture. Ask the audience what they see in the new image, and what the moves were that had to happen to achieve the ideal, with particular emphasis on the first moves that were made.

FEEDBACK AND DISCUSSION:

As above, the feedback from the audience to the group making the image is vital. What does each technique add to the story? How are the characters changing and developing? What new relationships become apparent? How is the story developing? Again, ask the audience first, and then the members of the group.

DEVELOPMENT:

The pictures created as images can be used in several ways, after the initial exploration of an issue. Here are just a few ideas:

- Create three pictures, showing the beginning, middle and end of a story. These can then be developed into a scene or scenes.

- Create a frozen picture of a conflict. Ask the audience what happened before this scene to create this picture. Then ask them to show this new image. What happened before this image? Create the new picture. Continue, until you have five or six images, building up a story. This can then be used to explore the individual images, or create scenes.

- Create images in pairs of, for example, parent and child. What is the situation? Where are they? Now improvise the scene.

- Create contrasting images of: the actual situation; the ideal situation; a character's fears; a character's hopes. Create a drama based on these.

- One person can sculpt the rest of a small group into their personal response to a word or issue. Offer each person this chance, then compare and contrast.

- Different groups can create different images of the same theme, which can then be compared.

Figure 2.3 Sculpting

10. The Forum Technique

Forum breaks down the barrier between actors and audience by presenting a problem on stage and inviting audience members to suggest and try out their own solutions, with the aim of changing the outcome. As a theatre form it demands active participation by the audience and assumes that the solutions to their problems can best be found by them. It is possible to create a full theatre piece and forum the decisions in that piece, but you can also forum scenes, or role play solutions in separate groups. At Leap, we use the forum technique as a training exercise, enabling young people to utilise their own power to change their life situation.

The following offers you an introduction to the forum technique.

Time:	This can take the form of a three-hour session or one/two days work.
Number in Group:	Minimum of 6
Aim:	To create a short piece of forum theatre with a group of young people.

DIRECTIONS:

(a) Creating the piece:

Assuming you have already decided on the issue of the piece, divide the group into smaller groups of no less than three or four. Ask group members to share personal stories about an experience of this issue when they felt powerless, remembering to maintain personal responsibility for information shared. It could be a story drawn directly from their lives or one which they have heard, which resonated for them.

Each group decides on using one person's story, or maybe creating a new story which incorporates elements of all their stories. Clarify that this is not a judgement on which is 'the best' story, but a search for the story which people identify with most, and feel a personal investment in.

Ask each group to build three or four still images of the story, perhaps representing the beginning, middle and end of the story. Explain that the group now has ownership of the story, rather than the individual, and that alterations can be made if need be.

Improvise around the images and build them into scenes.

(b) Rehearsing:

When the pieces have been largely worked out, it helps to share them with the larger group to focus the story and make sure they work as forum pieces. Ask the following questions of the audience:

- Do we understand the story?

- Is there a central character (the protagonist)?

- Are they oppressed?

- Do we care about them? If not, why not?

- Is it clear what the protagonist wants?

- Is there an identifiable antagonist (someone who embodies and maintains the oppression of the protagonist)?

- Is there room for intervention (i.e. someone from the audience attempting to change the outcome)?

Hear responses from the audience first, then ask the actors to respond. Give the groups time to rework their scenes, responding to the feedback from the audience. (For examples of rehearsal techniques *see* Unit Three.)

(c) Forum:

When the pieces are ready, you can forum them within the larger group or, if appropriate, invite in another group of young people to be the audience. The forum needs the role of a facilitator to introduce the piece and act as the link between the actors and the audience (*see* Notes below). The facilitator explains the rules and tells the audience that the piece will be run through twice. On the first run, they watch what happens and follow the actions of the central character. On the second run, the audience are invited to call out 'stop' when they have an intervention to make which they think will change the outcome for the central character. They then come on stage and take over the role of the central character and try out their intervention. The other actors remaining on stage improvise their response to the intervention, staying true to their characters and trying to maintain the original oppression. When the intervention is complete, the facilitator affirms the person for their intervention and asks them if they achieved what they wanted to. The facilitator asks the audience whether the intervention was a success or failure and why. Was it what the original character wanted? Was it magic – that is, could it really happen, or was the solution fantastical? The facilitator asks questions and provokes thought. The audience decides at which point to restart the piece and the original actors continue until the next intervention is made. Continue like this to the end of the piece or until you have run out of time. Stress that a solution is not the only aim, but a better understanding of real life and discovering potential points of change.

FEEDBACK AND DISCUSSION:
Reflect with the group on the different strategies explored during the forum, deepening the debate which the piece inspired. What skills are needed for different interventions? Do you have them? If not, how can you go about acquiring those skills? Are there other factors which, if in place, would facilitate a change? Are these achievable?

NOTES:
For the forum piece to be successful it needs to have certain components. It will help the group creating the scenes to use these as reference points during the devising process. These components are:

- The protagonist (a central character) – who the audience will identify with.

- An identifiable antagonist (the character who embodies the oppression).

- A potential ally – this character may be a friend, a parent etc. who offers the central character an opening to create change.

- A changeable outcome – it is vital that the piece has the potential for change and does not reinforce a feeling of powerlessness. For this reason, a situation of violence may not be suitable for forum, as the central character's alternatives are limited when their life is threatened.

- The facilitator – this role is crucial in moving the forum on, but not leading. The facilitator makes sure the power is in the hands of the audience, always referring to them to make decisions about the interventions and what point to start from.

Points to watch out for:

- The audience should only take on the role of the central character. They may wish to take over the role of the antagonist, in order to change the outcome, but the problem has to be addressed through changing our own actions.

- When an audience member intervenes, make sure they do not simply change the motivation of the original character as this would serve no purpose. Likewise, if the central character is disabled, then you cannot simply take away their disability. This is one reason why forum works best with a homogeneous group who identify with the oppression experienced by the central character.

- The role of the antagonist is a difficult one. When the intervention is made, the actor should aim to maintain the oppression. However, it is important that they find a balance between this aim as the character and the overall aim of the forum to explore potential change.

ENGENDERING LEADERSHIP: TRAINING IN WORKSHOP SKILLS (see also The Facilitator's Guide; Devising The Workshop, Unit Three)

A vital part of the training process for the young people is equipping them with workshop facilitation skills which they can use during the project and develop for future work. The workshop is as important as the performance, in terms of its educative value for the audience, offering an active exploration of the issues and deepening their response to the piece. The workshop also contributes to the breaking down of traditional barriers between audience and performers and involves both parties in the learning process. Facilitating the workshop increases the trainees' confidence and sense of empowerment, as they are in a position of responsibility, communicating directly with the recipients and seeing the impact of their work. This peer education approach draws on shared language and experiences to enhance the learning opportunity that exists.

Workshop leadership requires training and practice to ensure effective work is carried out. It is easy to put this to the side, seeing it as less of a priority than the immediacy of the performance. However, the more practice the group members get and the more opportunity to break down the workshop skills, the more skilfully they will manage the workshop. The following exercises are a framework for this training.

1. Working with Young People

(a) Concerns

Time:	30 minutes
Materials:	Flipchart paper, pens
Aim:	A small group exercise to provide the trainees with an appropriate space to think about working with young people.

DIRECTIONS:

Ask the group to divide into three smaller groups. Give each group ten minutes to brainstorm one question each:

- Why do a workshop?

- What are your concerns about running a workshop?

- What do you think the young people's concerns are?

FEEDBACK AND DISCUSSION:

Each group feeds back to the main group, and members of other groups, and you can add anything that is missing. Are there similarities between your concerns and the young people's concerns? If so, how might this help you in your work? What difference does being aware of young people's concerns make to your work?

(b) Boundaries

Time:	One hour
Material:	Flipchart paper, pens
Aim:	To explore the boundaries that are essential to good practice facilitation.

DIRECTIONS:

Brainstorm the following questions with your group.

- Why do you need boundaries when working with young people?

- What are appropriate boundaries to have?

Divide the group into three smaller groups. Ask each group to think of an 'unboundaried' response to a workshop situation – for example, disclosing an inappropriate personal experience when a young person is sharing their feelings about an event in their lives. Give each group ten minutes to role play their chosen situation.

Share the role plays with the whole group and use the forum technique to explore alternative responses (*see* The Forum Technique, Unit Two).

2. Workshop Styles

Time:	30–40 minutes
Aim:	An exercise to highlight effective facilitation styles through role play.

DIRECTIONS:
Brainstorm all the games the group have learnt so far.

Ask people to choose a game they feel confident to run with the rest of the group. Give each person a style to run the game in, which they don't tell the rest of the group. One by one, each person runs the game in the style. Examples of appropriate styles are: low energy, unplanned, unclear, cruel, aggressive, over-sympathetic, patronising, quiet, rushed. The rest of the group participate as themselves in the game.

FEEDBACK AND DISCUSSION:
After each game, disclose the style to the whole group and then ask for feedback on how they experienced that style. How did the different styles affect whether they understood the instructions or felt safe or were interested in the activity? What did they need in order to feel safe or interested? Be sure to provide clear boundaries for the feedback, emphasising that it is a game specifically to highlight different styles and not to criticise the people running the game. Remember to keep feedback focused and constructive.

NOTE:
This exercise uses negative aspects of facilitation to highlight the positive skills needed, but it is possible to set positive styles as well.

3. Roles in a Hat

Time:	20 minutes preparation time and 20 minutes per facilitation team
Materials:	Paper and pen, a hat

Aim: To use role play to demonstrate potential responses
                            of young people taking part in the workshop.

DIRECTIONS:

Divide the group into pairs. Ask each pair to plan the first ten minutes of a
workshop for young people, having agreed the setting. Decide on the
introduction and games played and who's running/saying what.

Ask for two volunteers to run their section. Give the rest of the group roles
as young people that they might encounter in that setting. For example, in a
youth club, someone who:

- wants to play pool
- loves drama
- is disruptive
- is interested but timid
- is worried about their image but interested
- thinks they know better
- fancies the workshop leader.

The first pair run their section, followed by feedback. Swap leaders and give
different group roles.

FEEDBACK AND DISCUSSION:

Ask each pair of facilitators to feedback to the group their experience of
running the section. What was difficult? What was easy? How did you work
together? How did you address any problems? What would you do differently?

Out of role, ask group members to feedback on how they experienced the
workshop. Were they engaged? Did they feel bored, scared or excluded for any
reason? How could this have been addressed?

NOTES:

Be careful when running this exercise to emphasise that the function of the
roles is to assist the training of the workshop leaders and not deliberately to
obstruct them. If necessary allocate the roles appropriately to individuals, for
example giving a quiet role to someone who might normally be disruptive (see
Role Work, Unit Two).

4. Running Small Sections

Time: 15 minute sections

Materials: Variable

Aim: To practise running a workshop in a safe and supportive atmosphere.

DIRECTIONS:

Divide the group into pairs. Each pair decides on two or three games that they want to try facilitating, thinking about the function of the games, for example energisers for warm-ups, massage for relaxation etc.

Each pair runs the workshop section, which the rest of the group participate in, as themselves, followed by feedback.

FEEDBACK AND DISCUSSION:

Ask the facilitators what they thought worked well, and what they could have improved. Then ask the group to feedback what they did well and why. Were the instructions clear? Did you enjoy the choice of games? How could they improve their facilitation?

NOTES:

This exercise can be run as a whole block of work, but it is equally useful to offer people the chance to run sections as part of the warm-up of a session, giving you a breathing space as well.

Ensure that all feedback is given in a positive and constructive manner.

5. Co-Leading

Time: 15 minutes

Materials: Flipchart paper, pens

DIRECTIONS:

Brainstorm the skills and qualities needed to co-lead a workshop. For example: listening skills, negotiation skills, support, communication skills, honesty, encouragement etc.

FEEDBACK AND DISCUSSION:

What are the practical ways in which you can improve co-leading? Encourage your group to think about creating enough planning time, clearly defining who is running what section, timing the workshop appropriately, developing signals with each other to ask for help, leaving time for evaluation etc.

This concludes Unit Two which has covered training your group in theatre and drama skills, group work and workshop facilitation as well as furthering the exploration of the issue. The next stage in the project is devising the theatre piece and the workshop.

3 THE RUN UP

OPPORTUNITY
TO FIND AND EXPRESS YOUR VOICE
RISKING REJECTION

UNIT THREE

THE RUN-UP

After we have prepared ourselves through training, we can start making the run-up to *the leap*. Now we have the skills and the confidence to take firm steps in the right direction and build the necessary momentum.

Unit Three: Devising the Show

UNIT GUIDE

Introduction
Devising a Theatre Piece
Aims of the Work
A Framework for Educational Theatre
Rehearsals
Presentation
The Workshop

INTRODUCTION

This is the point when the group is ready to start devising, drawing on their research, their shared experiences and their training in theatre and drama skills, to create a play which is their own and which can speak to an audience. It is a process of growth and change, where some material may be discarded or radically altered and where creativity can become blocked. However, it is also an exciting time, as the group expresses its vision and values, and learns how to shape the material it has generated into an accessible, educative and entertaining show. This section takes you through the process that Leap has developed, but there are other approaches to devising, including working with a writer, that you could explore. **We recommend that you read through the whole unit before beginning work.**

DEVISING A THEATRE PIECE

At Leap we have found that, when working with a large group, it is not appropriate to create a traditional play with a story that follows one central character from A to B. Instead, we create a piece of theatre that can employ a large cast, follow several characters' stories in parallel and draw on several styles, especially popular forms. Young audiences have a sophisticated grasp of visual performance from television and film as well as theatre, and will follow flashbacks and cuts into scenes outside the central characters' stories that comment on the issues in a different way, so don't be afraid to experiment.

We usually aim to devise a show of about 40 minutes, that is an ensemble piece, with no 'stars', using the performers' bodies and voices to create place or mood rather than elaborate sets. The piece is devised through scenes shaped in small groups of three to five people, but also with some scenes developed by the whole group. They improvise material which they then hone down and develop, bearing in mind the questions of audience and content, and they feedback on each other's work. The flexibility of the 'empty space' coupled with the rich input of the participants' research and personal experiences, creates an exciting piece of theatre that informs and entertains its audience.

AIMS OF THE WORK

Before they start creating the theatre piece, the group will need to think about both the general aims of educational theatre, and the more specific aims of this particular piece.

This should be a consultative process, so that the group continues to feel ownership of, and responsibility for, the work.

1. Aims of Educational Theatre

Time:	10 minutes
Materials:	Flipchart, pen
Aims:	To consider the aims of educational theatre.

DIRECTIONS:

As a whole group, brainstorm the aims of educational theatre. Who is its audience? Why present issues through theatre and not some other form?

Some replies might include:

- To bring about a change of consciousness
- To inform and educate
- To entertain (not necessarily to be comic)
- To show stories that resonate for young people
- To see and learn new responses to situations
- For the audience to see some theatre
- To make theatre that is specific to its audience
- To voice concerns of young people to decision makers

- To bring a subject to life and make it real and accessible
- To provoke debate
- To be young people-centred.

NOTE:
There is a strong history of educational theatre in the UK, and several books have been written about method and practice which you may find useful to read (*see* Resources).

2. Aims of this Particular Piece

Time:	10 minutes
Materials:	Flipchart, pen
Aims:	To consider together the aims of the theatre piece.

DIRECTIONS:
Leading on from the exercise above, brainstorm with the whole group what they are aiming to achieve in this piece.

Examples might include:

- To tell 'my' story
- To raise awareness of this particular issue
- To explore responses to a situation
- To tell it like it is, not how they say it is
- To show the issues theatrically
- To offer peer education
- To see several people's stories and experiences
- To elicit a reaction which can then be explored in the workshop
- To transform difficult personal experiences into learning ones for others.

A FRAMEWORK FOR EDUCATIONAL THEATRE
Audience, Content and Form

Once the group have agreed their aims for the piece, they can look in more detail at these three vital elements of theatre, in order to reflect what they want to say in an interesting, watchable way. Audience, content and form can be expressed as a triangular symbol (*see* Figure 3.1).

Exploring THE ISSUE
|
gives rise to THE THEME
|
which illustrates THE NARRATIVE THROUGHLINE

Figure 3.1 Three vital elements of theatre

That is, each component is an equal part of the whole, and all three must inter-relate to create the overall structure: you can't consider one without considering the others, and the group will need constantly to refer to these to make sure they are doing what they originally intended to do.

The Triangle

Time:	One hour
Materials:	Flipchart, pen
Aims:	To consider and agree as a whole group the audience, content and form of the piece before starting devising.

DIRECTIONS:

(a) Audience:
As a whole group brainstorm who the audience for this piece of theatre will be, considering for example age and gender, and where the audience will be: in schools, youth clubs, drop-in centres, or a combination of these. Will the audience be accustomed to seeing theatre? How might this affect them as an audience? What are their concerns? What issues are they interested in? From whose viewpoint? You may wish to review your earlier brainstorm sheets around working with young people.

Emphasise that when they are devising, they should constantly be referring back to their audience, and asking themselves is the piece:

- suitable (issues, language)?
- accessible (information and facts)?
- interesting (entertaining and educational)?

(b) Content:

(i) Review all the earlier brainstorm sheets that have been produced about the issue over the training period and all the material that has been generated. Allow the group some time to redigest this information.

(ii) Divide the group into three smaller groups, and ask each group to list what they want to say in the piece – what are their main concerns, and what do they think are the most important issues and/or facts that have come out of their research and the sharing of stories? Were there any particular pieces of information that stood out that they feel are vital?

(iii) Bring the whole group back together. Ask one group to feedback what they came up with and write it up on the flipchart. Ask the other two groups in turn what they listed: you will find that there are many crossovers and you may be able to group them under suitable headings, as well as list anything else they have thought of.

Ask the group whether they are happy with the final list of contents, and remind them to refer to it when devising to make sure they have covered the essentials. This might also be a good time to point out that maybe not every single last piece of information may be used, and that some things may have to be discarded in the interests of making a concise piece of theatre. However, all their main concerns should be addressed within the piece.

(c) Form:

Having agreed who they are performing to, and what they want to say, the group now needs to address how they are going to say it.

Working with the whole group, review the techniques they have learnt over the training period through brainstorming, and point out that they can draw on any of these when devising: images, machines, narrator, sound, song, music. These can spark creative ideas in people as they start to improvise, whilst also ensuring that they are not simply creating a naturalistic soap opera.

Issue, Theme and Narrative Throughline

It is worthwhile at this stage in the project to distinguish between the issue of the piece, for example drug use, and the main emerging theme which has arisen throughout the course of your exploration and action research, for example pressure. Establishing and developing the theme can provide the narrative throughline which holds the theatre piece together, offering you the necessary foundation on which to build a show with many layers and depth.

Our experience at Leap would suggest that the best way forward is for the facilitators to take the lead in proposing ideas for the narrative throughline and to think through their potential prior to taking them to the group. This will allow you some focused time to vision the piece, use your skills and experience to benefit the work and offer the group a viable idea to work with. Leaving it completely open to them can often be more disempowering and daunting than suggesting an idea and can also result in a compromised aesthetic. Be open, firm and honest with the group about your role in the process but do not undermine their responsibility for the work at this stage. Make it clear that you are bringing a suggestion to them and that it is for them ultimately to decide on it or discard it if they really want to.

1. Facilitator's Preparation

Discuss with your co-facilitator what has emerged from the weeks of training and action research. A theme may have emerged organically for the group, or you may need to brainstorm between you (or by yourself) the themes that have been dominant and/or that you feel have great theatrical potential.

Once you have identified the theme, you then need to explore how you can draw on it to hold the piece together. You could again brainstorm the theme to see what words, thoughts and associations arise. Is there a visual image that the theme conjures up that you could illustrate on stage? Is there a piece of music which expresses the sentiments of the theme?

Other possibilities: if a strong theme does not emerge or if you decide not to use it as a conceptual thread, here are a number of narrative devices which you can draw on to create the throughline of the play. You could:

(a) use a neutral narrator to speak directly to the audience, take us through the different characters' stories and comment on the action

(b) create a character to function as a narrator

(c) introduce a reporter or investigator who is investigating the issue and is taken through the play alongside the audience. His/her comments after scenes can then link the different characters' stories

(d) invent a place where all the characters meet, such as a homeless hostel, a drugs project or a classroom. This could either be at the beginning of the play (and we then rewind to hear their stories) or at the end of the play. They could know each other, or just be in the same place without their paths crossing

(e) create an incident which impacts on all the characters, then show their stories unfold through the action.

Decide on one or two ideas that you feel are most appropriate and that you feel the group will be happy with.

2. Bringing Ideas to the Group

You need to bring these ideas to the group. However, at this early stage of devising it is not necessary to spend a great deal of time working out and discussing the throughline of the piece as you want the group to focus on creating the characters' stories. You could decide to hold a discussion based on the theme after some material has been created and then slowly, over the course of the character work, feed in your idea for the narrative throughline. This is important so that the group can begin to picture the whole, and have an understanding of what they are working towards. This will help to motivate group members in times of anxiety and frustration during the devising process (which are inevitable). Give the group time to digest and discuss the throughline of the piece and to 'give it the go-ahead'. Be open and flexible to changes that they want to make in the process of owning this.

Tension and Atmosphere

Whatever level of experience you are bringing to directing the devised piece, there are certain elements that you need to bear in mind when creating a piece of theatre that will make it more effective dramatically. Dramatic tension, or suspense, is what keeps an audience interested in the piece and committed to watching it – it is the subconscious question we ask when watching drama, 'What happens next?', and is what keeps us hooked. When the groups are creating the scenes for the story, they need to think about how an audience would respond, if seeing it for the first time. How do you build a sequence of events towards a climax or resolution? Where do you end a scene to ensure that the audience are going to want to know what happens next? How could sound or silence, or movement add to the tension?

Another dramatic tool is atmosphere, inducing a feeling or mood in the audience and making settings believable. This is especially important in live performance. For example, if a scene is set in a courtroom, get the group to think about what kind of atmosphere there is in court – reverent, hushed, solemn etc. How can you create or enhance the mood, for example through music or sound?

As the director, you have the benefit of an outside eye and can imagine how an audience might respond. This can help you guide the group towards creating the piece.

Rhythm and Pace

The rhythm of a scene is about whether the dialogue follows everyday speech patterns of question and answer, interruptions, chunks of speech and so on. When the groups show their scenes, make a point of listening to the speech patterns, to see if anything jars, whether the timing of responses sounds right, whether it is too fast or too slow.

Pace is a very important element of theatre, both for contrast and for maintaining interest, both within a scene and between scenes, and will elicit responses in the audience accordingly. For example, the audience will need time to digest a fast scene full of information, so the following scene will need to be slower and quieter as a contrast. Deciding the pace of particular scenes can partly be done at the devising stage, but will be most obvious once you have seen the whole piece and can juxtapose the scenes accordingly. There can also be a tendency for the pace to slow down as the piece progresses, so encourage the group to keep the pace ticking over so that the audience do not get bored. This means ensuring that cues are picked up quickly, and that changes from one scene to another are done efficiently.

Character Work

Creating characters forms a central part of the devising process. Real and empathetic character stories, which a youth audience can identify with, will make or break the success of the theatre piece. The conflicts faced by the characters and the decisions they make need to be believable and relevant to sustain the interest of the audience. The characters bring the issue dealt with by the play to life and ensure that the audience engages on an emotional, as well as intellectual, level.

In Leap's devising process, we have found that three character stories is a good number to work with for a number of reasons:

- It allows us to address a range of circumstances and deal with different issues and outcomes.

- It allows us to present characters from different cultures, ethnic backgrounds and genders which reflect the diversity of the audience membership.

- It offers a number of substantial roles for a large group.

- It allows the whole group to work in three smaller teams, which ensures contributions from everyone and produces more material at a faster rate!

Creating a Character

Discuss with the group the reasons for choosing three character stories, that is, the opportunities it offers the group. There are a number of different starting points for building characters, all of which offer the group the opportunity to draw on experiences from their own lives and the learning of the action research they have undertaken. It is important to remember the aim of the piece and to bear it in mind throughout the character development. Remind the group that the characters are their tools with which to make their statement about the issue.

1. The Character Outline

Time: 45 minutes

Aim: To create three characters for the play.

DIRECTIONS:

Use a brainstorm as your starting point. For example, if you are looking at drug use, brainstorm why young people use drugs or if the piece is about home-lessness, brainstorm why young people become homeless.

Ask the group to divide into three groups and each to choose one of the words or phrases from the brainstorm. (Make sure they take a different word each.) In their groups, suggest they do another brainstorm around their chosen word to deepen their thoughts on the subject before continuing. Now ask them to create a frozen picture with a central character, which illustrates their response to that word. Encourage them to do this in silence without preparation, communicating through their body images not through words. Go around the groups and use Touch and Tell (see Image Work, Unit Two) to find out more about the picture. After creating the image, ask the groups to decide the following:

- Who is the central character?

- What is their name?

- How old are they?

- Where do they live?

VARIATIONS:

Other ways to create the characters include:

(a) Decide on a setting where everyone is, depending on the issue you are addressing. For example, it could be a day centre for homeless people if the issue is homelessness, or a school classroom if it is bullying. Disclose the setting to the group and ask participants to decide for themselves on their own character and why they are at this particular place. What is their name? Where are they from? Who are their family? What has just happened to them? How long have they been in this place? How are they feeling now? Ask them to create a still image of how they are feeling now.

Share four or five of the images at the same time with the rest of the group and touch and tell each image, for the group to find out more about the characters. Ask the 'audience' to select one of the images from the four or five seen that they would like to develop further, using a voting system to decide which one.

Repeat this with another four or five of the images, again selecting one image to work with. Repeat this a third time with the rest of the unseen images.

You should now have three selected images from the whole group that everyone has agreed to use as the three main characters of the play.

Stress the importance for group members, when selecting, to vote for one that they identify with and that resonates for them, also bearing in mind the need for variety within the three characters.

(b) Give each group a different bag of objects (eg. a train ticket, a necklace, a baseball cap, a photograph) and ask them to create the owner of the objects, through discussion.

(c) Give each group a photograph of a person. Decide who they are. Build up a character profile from the picture.

FEEDBACK AND DISCUSSION:

Bring the whole group back together and share the three characters they have created. This promotes shared ownership of the characters and provides an opportunity to make changes to the characters if necessary, in order to adhere more closely to the aims of the piece. You may wish to reflect on the characters' ages, ethnicity, class, family situation etc. and make alterations. Keep the discussion focused and ensure that people are being sensitive to each other and not phrasing suggestions as criticisms.

NOTES:

When the groups are creating the characters, you have the overview. You may need to encourage one group to alter their circumstances if they are too similar to another group's, or to use a different participant to play the role if you realise that all the characters are the same ethnicity or gender. Refer back to the aim of the piece to support your decision to encourage changes. Undertaking this process at this point means you are less likely to have changes to make later on. If a larger issue arises, for example they have created a character who has been sexually abused, you may decide to bring it back to the whole group to discuss the appropriateness of addressing this issue within this context, and the sensitivity needed with a youth audience. Raise the reasons for addressing it, that is, to raise awareness, to confront the taboo surrounding the issue, to show support for young people who may have experienced abuse, to inform them of possible courses of action, as well as the concerns, that is, the feelings it may bring up for some children and the lack of support available in schools, and the need for follow-up work. Be structured and sensitive in your discussion, and remember, do not assume anything – you may well have people in the group who have these experiences.

2. Developing the Character

Now you have created the outline of the character, it is important to flesh them out, developing their background, their relationships, their characteristics, their status level etc. Here are a selection of exercises you could use to develop the characters further. The first three exercises are for small groups to work on the three main characters, whereas the last two exercises are to be used more generally when all group members have a character to develop.

(a) Character History

Time:	45 minutes
Aim:	To create the characters' life histories.

DIRECTIONS:

In groups of three, decide on four important points in the characters' lives (each group taking one character to work on) that have significance in relation to who they are now. For example, mother and father split up when the character was five years old, moved to new town when eight, mother remarried, left home at fifteen. Create a fifth image of the character in the present. Practise moving from one image to the next in a sequence.

FEEDBACK AND DISCUSSION:

Share the sequences with the whole group. Touch and tell (*see* Image Work, Unit Two). Clarify any confusions which arise from any of the sequences so, once again, the whole group are involved in developing the characters and have a sense of their histories.

NOTE:

This process is to discover background information on the character and is not necessarily material to be used in the play.

(b) Hotseating

Time:	30 minutes
Aim:	To help the person playing the character create a personality and gain the characters sense of 'self'.

DIRECTIONS:

Invite each character one by one (or if you are short of time ask all three characters simultaneously) to sit in the 'hotseat' and answer questions from the rest of the group. For example: what is a happy memory from your childhood? What do you want to achieve in your life? How do you get along with your family?

In order to derole the group member, applaud them after they have finished in role, and say their real name, welcoming them back to the group (*see* Role Work, Unit Two).

NOTES:

Stress that the aim of this exercise is to help the person build the character and not to catch them out if they contradict themselves. Encourage the group to ask questions about feelings as well as events. You may wish to limit group members to one or two questions each to allow everyone a chance to ask a question.

This is a useful preparation for the workshop, as you may well decide to use hotseating as a part of the final event (*see also* Devising the Workshop, Unit Three).

(c) Building a Picture

Time:	45 minutes
Aim:	To develop the emotional nature of the character.

DIRECTIONS:

In three groups (each group taking one character to work on), create images for each of the following:

(i) the character's biggest fear

(ii) the character's greatest secret

(iii) the character's greatest hope

(iv) what makes the character sad

(v) what makes the character angry.

FEEDBACK AND DISCUSSION:

Share the images with the whole group. Touch and tell. What emotions do the different characters have in common? What are the differences? How might these emotions affect their relationships and their actions?

NOTE:

As with all image work, encourage the group to think physically and not to discuss it too much.

Figure 3.2 Character work

(d) A Day in the Life of

Time:	30 minutes
Aim:	To develop the character further by inventing a day in their life.

DIRECTIONS:

Prepare the group for this activity by asking them to find a space on their own, lie down and shut their eyes and focus on the character they are playing. When you feel people are ready, ask them, in role, to mime a day in the life of their character, beginning from waking up in the morning. Encourage them to act out in detail the character's everyday activities. Do they eat breakfast, wash, work, see friends, go shopping, meet people, watch television etc.? Get them to think about their character's status and tension level (*see* States of Tension and Status, Unit Two).

FEEDBACK AND DISCUSSION:

Bring the group together to share their experiences. Did they learn anything new about the character through this exercise? What is their character's natural status and tension level? Is it different from their own? How difficult was it to stay focused? How might this relate to performing? What skills do they need to overcome these difficulties?

(e) Animal Characters

Time:	30 minutes
Aim:	To develop the characters' physicality.

DIRECTIONS:

Prepare the group for the following exercise by playing a round of animal tag (*see* Games, Unit One). Ask the group to find a space on their own, lie down and shut their eyes and focus on the character they are playing. Ask them to think about what kind of animal their character would be. Are they quiet and shy? Proud? Angry and upfront? Offer possibilities – would they be a snake, a horse, a monkey, an eagle, a bear, a cat, a tiger, a tortoise? Once they have decided, ask them to move around the room as the animal. Does it move fast or slow? How does it feed? How does it interact with other animals? Is it confident? What does it want? Encourage them to try different things until they feel comfortable and to exaggerate their movements and sounds. Give them time to develop their ideas.

DEVELOPMENT:

Ask everyone to return to the human character they were originally playing, but retain one or two characteristics from the animal such as the way they walk, or a way of holding their head. In three smaller groups place the characters in a situation (eg. a hostel, a party, a drop-in, a doctor's waiting room) and ask them to improvise a short scene, exhibiting the animal characteristics.

FEEDBACK AND DISCUSSION:

In a whole group discuss if and how this exercise has developed the characters they are playing. Did they find it difficult? Why? How might it help when they are working on the scenes? Affirm them for having done this exercise – it requires confidence, a positive attitude and a focused mind.

NOTES:

Certain members may need help deciding on an animal. Also, individuals may find this exercise very difficult and embarrassing, so be aware of this and do more preparation if necessary. However, it does create a challenge for the participants and can stretch their boundaries and expand the dimension of the characters they create. It is also useful to refer to these animals when rehearsing later on to develop the scenes.

The Characters' Scenes

As well as working with three characters, we have found that creating three scenes for each character provides a solid framework for the stories to develop with a clear beginning, middle and an end. It also allows each of the characters time to undertake a believable process of change within the course of a 40–50 minute play. Once again, it is important to think about the aims of the piece when developing the three scenes. What do you want to say about the issue? What understanding do you want the audience to walk away with? Do you want to show how young people can overcome a problem, or to show how overwhelming the oppression is? Do you want to end the performance with a cliffhanger decision to be made which can be followed up in the workshop? As stated earlier, using three characters gives you the freedom to illustrate a number of different outcomes. With the aim of empowerment in mind, the young people working at Leap usually choose to show the characters beginning to overcome the oppression they are facing in the third scene, although no 'easy solutions' are presented. In this way, the audience (who are often facing the same oppressions as the characters in the play) can reflect on their own situations and see different strategies working for others, giving them a sense of hope and possibility for their futures.

A template structure for the three scenes is as follows:

Scene One: The character's situation/oppression is introduced to the audience.

Scene Two: The character is at their lowest ebb – crisis point.

Scene Three: The character makes a positive step towards change

or

The character becomes more entrenched in their circumstances. There is a way out implied in the scene but the character does not recognise it, although the audience might.

1. Making Scene One

Time: Dependent on the length of your devising period.

Minimum time: 1–2 hours per scene

Aim: To create the first character scene for the play.

DIRECTIONS:

Divide the group into three smaller groups, with three group members playing the three characters that you have already created in a different group. Discuss the aims of the introductory scene with your group: to present the character, to highlight their dilemma, to find out something about their background, their age, class, home-life etc.

Ask them to make a frozen picture of the first time the audience meets the character. Now ask them to decide what happens next and to create two more frozen pictures which illustrate the middle and the end of the scene. Once these three frozen pictures are created, the group will have established the structure of their scene and can begin improvising, using movement and dialogue, to bring the scene to life. Give them a set amount of time to achieve this before showing the scenes to the whole group. Each scene should last about three minutes.

FEEDBACK AND DISCUSSION:

Sharing the scenes and receiving feedback on them is a vital part of the devising process. It has three main functions:

(a) To encourage shared ownership of the different stories.

(b) To keep focused on the whole of the play and to address how the scenes fit together.

(c) To increase group members' ability to critique a piece of theatre, and offer positive and constructive feedback.

You may wish to structure the feedback session around specific questions which exclude negative comments. For example: what things did you think worked well? How could the group improve the scene? Was the story clear? Let the group members watching feedback first, and then offer the group performing a chance to reflect on what they've heard and the problems they encountered when devising the scene. You need to address both the theatricality of the scene and the educational content in the feedback. Were the issues raised in an accessible way for young people? Was it informative? What could they add to make it more educational? Applaud each group to keep the atmosphere affirmative, bearing in mind how exposed and vulnerable people can feel when performing in front of others.

DEVELOPMENT:

Now ask the groups to rework the scenes, building in the feedback they have received. Point out that some potentially exciting material may have to be discarded, simply to make the scene work more effectively. Then hold another sharing and feedback session, so that this honing down of material becomes a natural and intrinsic part of the devising process. When you feel the scenes are ready, provide the groups with flipchart, pen and paper to record the main elements of the scenes and any good lines that they may wish to remember.

NOTES:

Encourage the participants to be imaginative when building the scenes and to draw on the techniques they have learnt in Unit Two. The scenes work well when largely naturalistic, complementing the non-naturalistic nature of the interlinking scenes. However, they can contain freezes, machines, repeated voices and sounds to enhance their effectiveness and theatricality.

2. Making Scenes Two and Three

You can create Scenes Two and Three using the same approach as in Scene One, that is, use three frozen pictures to give the structure and then improvise the action around this. It is important to change the make-up of the smaller groups for Scenes Two and Three, if you wish to introduce other characters into the scenes, and also to allow different participants to work together. Central characters should obviously be played by the same person in all three scenes.

3. The Ingredients of a Scene

It is helpful to provide your group with a check-list of the components of a scene for them to refer to whilst developing their stories. This will slowly become automatic as they gain more experience and understanding of the processes of theatre making. Our check-list is as follows – you may well have other points you wish to add:

(a) Beginning, Middle and End

Remind the group of the need for all stories to have a beginning, a middle and an end (Scenes One, Two and Three) and that each scene also needs these three points. This creates a very simple way to structure a scene, ensuring that there is a journey and a sense of development. Using frozen pictures for each of these points, as above, is an effective way of achieving a dramatic structure.

(b) The Five W's

Where is the scene taking place? *When*? *Who* are the characters? *What* do they want? *Why* do they want it? Make sure that the answers to these questions are explicit in the scene to ensure that the basic information required by the audience will be presented and not assumed to be obvious. It is amazing how easy it is not to reveal the place setting in the scene, which will leave the audience confused and uncertain of the situation. Clear indicators in scenes, such as a school bell ringing to mark the end of class, can inform the audience of the setting immediately.

(c) Conflict

Drama is about conflict. Observing the conflict as it emerges and is, perhaps, resolved engages the audience in the characters' stories. Is there a decision to be made? What stands in the way of the central character achieving what they want? Conflict does not always mean fighting and arguing between characters. The conflict could be an internal one, or it could be underlying in the scene and not outwardly expressed. It heightens the tension of the piece, and propels the story forward.

(d) The Main Character's Thoughts and Feelings

What often happens when exploring an oppression experienced by the central character is that they are silenced by the oppression and become a passive victim who 'has things done' to them. The outcome of this is often that the audience does not identify with the character or empathise with their situation as there is no window into their thoughts and feelings and they are perceived as 'weak'.

There are dramatic techniques which can counteract this, ensuring that the central character's voice is heard. These include:

(i) monologue – where the character speaks either to themselves (overheard by the audience) or directly to the audience sharing their feelings and thoughts.

(ii) diary/letters – the character writes entries into a diary or writes letters to a close friend, speaking out loud.

(iii) other actors play the voices in the head of the character.

Figure 3.3 Voices in the head technique

4. Changing the Dynamics (see also Rehearsals, Unit Three)

If a scene is lacking energy and tension, try using some of the exercises in Unit Two. Changing the status level of the characters or giving them different states of tension will provide you with a range of tools to utilise and encourage the group to 'play' with their material more and improve its quality.

Non-Character Scenes

The characters' histories, and the scenes exploring their dilemmas and responses, are the backbone of the piece, offering stories that are relevant to the audience, reflecting their own lives and concerns.

However, there will also be facts and figures, or related issues, that are not appropriate for exploration through these character stories. Alongside these character scenes, therefore, the group can now devise scenes that comment on the issues from other angles. This will also give those members of the group who are not playing large parts in the character scenes the chance to take larger parts here.

Moreover, the character scenes will probably develop in a fairly naturalistic way, and tend towards the serious rather than the humorous, so some other scenes, interspersed between the character scenes, that are comic and non-naturalistic will make the overall piece more varied and interesting.

At Leap, we find that these other scenes usually take the form of:

- presenting crucial facts and figures in a theatrical way

- exploring stereotyped images, as portrayed in the media

- commenting on the issue from a different perspective, using the whole group

- using case studies to create monologues.

These scenes are devised in parallel with the character scenes, so you are constantly generating material for the piece, whilst preventing the staleness that would occur if you only worked on one set of scenes.

1. Facts into Theatre

Time:	Minimum 1–2 hours
Aim:	To create scenes that present facts and statistics in a theatrically interesting way.

DIRECTIONS:

(a) Settings:
As a whole group, brainstorm possible settings for non-character scenes that can convey information essential to the theme. For example, work around homelessness inevitably raises issues relating to the Unemployment Office and the Housing Office. Whilst the character scenes may show specific characters attending these places, these non-character settings lend themselves to a commentary on the bureaucracy involved, and to offering important facts and/or statistics. Select the number of 'fact' scenes you require for the theatre piece: we usually work with three. Divide into the appropriate number of smaller groups ensuring that people are working in different groups to the character groups.

Each group then selects one of the settings to work with.

Give people any relevant factsheets or research that they have previously worked from. Each group then lists up to ten facts, gleaned from their research, that they consider to be important, and then selects the five most essential to convey in the piece.

(b) Styles / Genres:

Now that each group has agreed the five facts they want to communicate about a particular setting, they need to find an exciting way of saying it. A successful way of doing this is to devise the scene in a recognisable style or genre, making the presentation of potentially dry facts entertaining, theatrical and often humourous.

Bring the whole group back together and brainstorm all the different styles of theatre, film and television they can think of. For example:

Horror film	Pantomime
Film noir	Western
Advertisement	Game show
Children's theatre	Victorian melodrama
Sitcom	Restoration comedy
Jacobean tragedy	James Bond film
Soap opera	Documentary

Each group then selects a different style that they want to create their scene in, and then brainstorms the characteristics of that style, so that everyone is agreed on what effect they are trying to create.

For example, the characteristics of a western might be:

American accents	Saloon bars
Cowboys	Sheriff
A hero and a 'baddie'	Saloon girls
Whiskey drinking	

The small groups now start to devise their scenes, conveying their five chosen facts, in the style they have chosen, for example a scene set at the Housing Office, presented as a horror film. Again, these should last no longer than three minutes, and should aim to be comic. If the group finds it easier, ask them to structure the scene by creating images of the beginning, middle and end of the scene before linking it all together.

Give them a set amount of time to do this, before showing their work to the whole group. Make sure that you circulate among the groups, offering support and suggestions to help them in their devising.

VARIATIONS/DEVELOPMENT:

Encourage the groups to think about the music or sound associated with their chosen style, and incorporate this into their scene, for example *The Good, The*

Bad and The Ugly theme for a western, or a well-known game show theme tune for a quiz show. This will help the audience recognise the genre you are working with.

Other ways of generating material that can be presented using the different styles are:

- using a case study and selecting the main points the group wants to get across
- using a newspaper or magazine report and selecting the main points they want to convey.

FEEDBACK AND DISCUSSION:

These scenes usually work quite well from the start, and the groups will be encouraged by the response they get, but make sure that, alongside the questions they ask about what works successfully in the scene and why, the feedback addresses these questions:

- Did you understand what they were trying to say?
- What were the facts or pieces of information being conveyed?

Make sure that the style doesn't obscure the points they are trying to get across.

After the feedback session, the groups can continue to work on the scenes, honing the material, and write up the core action of the scene and any particularly good lines or moments that they want to remember.

NOTE:

The groups need to be familiar with the characteristics of the style they have selected, and also be sure that the audience will recognise the genre, for example most members of a youth club will probably not recognise the style of restoration comedy!

2. Exploring Stereotypes

We are all accustomed to the stereotyped images that surround certain themes and people in the media; for example, we are used to seeing headlines about 'the Scrounging Homeless' and visual images of old alcoholic men sleeping on the streets.

The theatre piece is an opportunity for the group to take a critical look at these images and explode some of the myths and stereotypes surrounding the theme for their audience, to highlight some of the assumptions we all make. This can be in scenes interspersed throughout the show, or created as one scene by itself.

Figure 3.4 The 'Dole Boys' run the benefit office

Time:	Initially 1–2 hours
Materials:	Newspapers or magazines that can be used as starting points. You may wish to ask the group to bring in any headlines or images that they have noticed that show stereotypes on the theme.
Aim:	To create scenes that expose stereotypes and myths about the selected theme.

DIRECTIONS:

If you have some images or headlines that you wish to use as triggers, show them to the group, but these are not vital.

As a whole group, brainstorm a list of 'Media myths and stereotypes about...' (the theme you are working with), for example: all people who take drugs are worthless junkies; all gay men are secret paedophiles; all unemployed people are scroungers who don't want to work. As a whole group, select a number of these that you wish to work with (say three to five). Divide the group into the same number of smaller groups, again mixing and matching group members.

Each group then selects one of these stereotypes each, and devises a scene to show that this myth or stereotype is just that. Encourage them to use humour, and to draw on all the techniques they have learnt in the training period, such as images, machines, narrators, captions and pictures, so that the scenes are stylised rather than naturalistic – exaggeration is a useful way of exposing absurdity. They may also wish to incorporate real or invented headlines.

The scenes can be very short, a couple of minutes at most, and you should move around the groups helping them to realise what they are trying to create. Give a set amount of time to work on the scenes, and then bring the whole group back together to show their work and feedback.

FEEDBACK AND DISCUSSION:

Was it clear what the stereotype or myth was? How did the group show it was a myth? What worked well, and how could the scene be improved?

The groups can then continue their work on the scenes, again writing down any memorable moments or lines and the structure of the scene.

VARIATIONS:

Divide the group into three smaller groups, and give each group the same list of five facts about someone affected by the issue. Each group then develops a scene, or a 'photo' and caption, from differing media/political viewpoints, such as three newspapers taking different stances on the issue. How does each paper treat the same facts? This will also give the group insight into how facts can be manipulated by the media for political purposes, which could be reflected in the theatre piece.

Alternatively, each group could interview a character, throwing questions at him/her from their political stance, or use physical theatre to show how an individual is affected by the stereotypes, caught between them or crushed by them, and how it affects others' views of them.

DEVELOPMENT:

There is a whole area of work that could be explored about stereotyping and the purpose it serves. For example, you could start by looking at the positive and negative aspects of the media (e.g. positive: an issue raised by the media will raise awareness of that issue; negative: the newspaper involved shows yet another stereotyped photographic image) and then go on to explore the positive and negative effects of the stereotypes around your selected theme (*see also* Notes below).

NOTE:

It is important to emphasise that the aim of these scenes is to expose the stereotype, not create or reinforce it. This can be clarified by encouraging the groups to spell out and exaggerate the stereotype they are working with and to make the scene humorous. This makes the scene much clearer for the audience, and highlights the absurdity of the accepted image.

3. Commenting on the Issue as a Whole Group (see also Image Work, Sound Pictures, Unit Two and Facts into Theatre, Unit Three)

This material should be developed slightly later in the devising process, as it will be informed by the character scenes and how the overall story is progressing. This is another time when it is a good idea for you as the facilitator to bring some suggestions to the group, as you have the overview. This means you can offer ideas for commenting on the issues from a different perspective using the whole group (e.g. loss of individuality in relation to bureaucracy) or creating a setting where it would be interesting to hear lots of different voices (e.g. the school playground in a piece about bullying). Moving images or machines are particularly useful techniques to use in this context.

Time: 1–2 hours

Aim: To devise a non-naturalistic scene, as a whole group, that comments on the theme.

DIRECTIONS:

Once you have agreed a subject for the scene, start by creating a sound circle.

Go round the circle, asking each person in turn to make a noise or say a line or phrase that relates to the theme. When everyone has got a sound, practise saying them individually in turn, and then simultaneously. For example, for a street scene:

First person: 'Good morning'

Second person: A car alarm or police siren

Third person: Asks to buy some apples

Now ask each person to add a movement to their sound, and repeat the sound and movement continuously. Next, practise moving together round the room, using the sounds and movements all together. Now number the group and call out different numbers, to vary the order of the different sounds and movements.

From this, you will be able to see a simple story for the scene emerging, as people's lines relate to one another and you can see characters emerging. Decide on an order for these, so that the scene starts to tell a story. Some people may need to adapt their movement or sound slightly, to clarify the story of the scene. The scene should build to a climax, perhaps by building the volume or pace of the sounds and movements; or perhaps the narrator enters at a suitable moment and ends the scene; or perhaps a signal is given to end the scene abruptly. Once you have the basis of a scene of two to three minutes you are all happy with, rehearse it several times.

VARIATIONS/DEVELOPMENT:

(a) Instead of movements and/or sounds that are created by individuals, you could agree movements and sounds that are repeated and coordinated by the whole group simultaneously.

(b) Divide the group into two groups, representing two groups within a scene, for example homeless people and passers-by. Each group develops a movement and/or sound which can then be directed into a scene.

(c) Divide the group into twos and threes; each small group creates a movement and/or sound together which is then directed into a short scene.

NOTE:

Listen to suggestions and emphasise that your role is as the outside eye, and that you may be able to see things that they cannot: this is now starting to become a piece of theatre, and you need to say honestly what seems to work well and what doesn't, whilst continuing to encourage contributions from the group.

4. Case Studies

Another option for non-character scenes is to create one or two monologues, drawing on case studies and the facts and figures discovered during research, bringing them to life. These can be very effective, especially when contrasted with large group scenes.

Figure 3.5 A group scene

Again, the devising of these scenes can come later on in the process, once you have a clearer idea of how the piece will be structured.

Time:	One hour
Aim:	To create one or two dramatic monologues, drawing on case studies.

DIRECTIONS:

As a whole group, decide who, at this point, might perform a monologue. These should preferably be those who are not playing a large part elsewhere, and who feel confident about speaking alone.

Ask for other people to work alongside them, one or two to accompany each person doing the monologue.

Give each of these small groups a case study to work from, which you should find in books and handbooks on such issues as drug use and homelessness. Ask them to create a speech from this, said in the first person, adding and editing where necessary.

For example, the facts of a case study: 'Tina was 17 when she first started using drugs' becomes: 'My name is Tina. I am 17 years old and have just tried Ecstasy for the first time'.

The other people in the group help create the monologue and then coach and direct the person performing it.

VARIATIONS/DEVELOPMENT:

Using different source material, the character performing the monologue could be someone outside the action, such as someone's mother giving their reaction, or a worker in a hostel. This could be scripted if required.

Other actors in the scene can enhance the monologues visual theatricality, for example each actor could repeat a movement, or say a word that comments on the monologue, rather like the 'Machine' exercise. (*see also* Machines, Unit Two.)

FEEDBACK AND DISCUSSION:

Ask the group whether the character, and what they want and why, is clear. Did the pace of the speech drop at any point? Is it the right length, or could it be longer or shorter?

Non-Character Scenes: Further Suggestions

These are some examples of scenes that you can develop alongside the character scenes. You can mix and match them, so that, for example, you explore media stereotypes as a whole group scene or as a monologue, and you can also link them together. Other possibilities include devising running gags in groups of two or three, like a music hall turn, or you could adapt the above exercises to focus on a specific aspect of your theme that needs exploring, such as the hopes and dreams of the characters, alongside the daily realities of their lives. You could also adapt children's games or rhymes to use in the piece.

Always refer back to the Audience, Content and Form triangle.

Opening Scene

At this stage you should have devised most of the other material for the play, have clarified what the throughline is and maybe some idea of the running order. Now return to the beginning and decide on the opening sequence which serves to introduce the audience to your imaginary world and to highlight what the play is about. Although it is most sensible to devise the opening scene at this late stage once the stories and theme have emerged, it is something that you will need to be thinking about throughout the course of the devising process.

Opening scenes can draw on Image Work, Machines and Sound Pictures (Unit Two) to create a suitable beginning for the play. It might be that having decided on using the theme as the narrative throughline, you will wish to create an image of this in the opening scene. Or you could open the play with harsh statistics on the issue which the characters' stories then highlight.

Decide on whether you want to have a high energy, loud start to grab the audience's attention (using music, drumming etc.) or whether you want to ease them in gently. At Leap, we often start the piece with a whole group scene, which raises the issue and establishes the ensemble nature of the piece. However, you may decide to introduce the audience to the characters first of all or to use a narrator to speak directly to the audience.

Closing Scene

The closing scene of the play has a range of potential functions:

- to sum up the events of the play
- to pose a key question which has been raised
- to offer a resolution to the conflicts of the play.

As in the opening scene, you can draw on Image Work, Machines and Sound Pictures (Unit Two), to create a suitable final scene.

One approach is to repeat the opening sequence but adapt it to highlight the changes that have happened in the play. This gives the piece a cyclical sense of completion.

Running Order

Now you need to return to the structure of the theatre piece. You are likely to have created nine character scenes and perhaps six or seven non-character scenes which address the issues in a different way. The first thing to do is list all the scenes with the group so they have an overview of the material they have created. It is a good idea for you to have prepared a rough idea of the running order, and to suggest it to the group for approval. An example of a suitable running order is as follows:

Opening Scene

Character (A) Scene 1

Character (B) Scene 1

Character (C) Scene 1

Group scene

Character (A) Scene 2

Character (C) Scene 2

Group scene

Character (B) Scene 2

Group scene

Character (C) Scene 3

Monologue

Group scene

Character (A) Scene 3

Character (B) Scene 3

Closing scene

Hear any concerns from the group in regard to your suggested running order and, once again, be flexible and open to trying it different ways and adapting it as you go along. Nothing is set in stone at this stage. The best way to see how it works is to run it through.

REHEARSALS

The group have agreed on the content and form, and devised and structured the material. They now have a piece of theatre – which, no doubt, needs substantial rehearsing! This is the stage when the participants learn how to rehearse and polish their piece, referring constantly to the audience – who is the audience? Where are they sitting? Is the play interesting to watch? Can the actors be seen and heard? As the director, you may be wondering how you can tighten up the show, so that it runs smoothly. How can you vary the pace? How can you help people learn their lines?

The participants are now making the transition into performers: many young people find the rehearsal process a challenging one, and they may become bored, distracted and unfocused. They are no longer inventing and creating material, but must go over the work several times, learn their lines, remember where they are standing in a particular scene and what they are doing, and remember how the scenes link together. They will need to learn the discipline of concentrating during rehearsals, so that they will remember all this, and get into the habit of focusing on the show regardless of how the audience is reacting. Continue to affirm their work, whilst developing their skills and building their confidence, maintaining your role as the supportive 'outside eye'. Be positive about all the effort they have made, and point out that the rehearsal process may be difficult, but that it is worth this extra push to ensure the success of the piece and so that they will be proud of their achievement.

You may wish to do some preparatory work with the group to prepare them for this stage of the process and some of the changes that will be taking place as they complete their run-up to the leap of the first performance.

1. The Facilitator as Director

As a facilitator, you will have noticed already how your role has subtly changed during the devising process, and this will continue during rehearsals as you take on more of a directing role rather than one of facilitation. You now have a responsibility to offer an outside artistic eye on the work, and to explain why something won't seem clear to an audience; to offer support to the cast; and to set clear guidelines and boundaries for the rehearsal process. You and the group will need to adjust to your different role, but as long as you are clear what you are doing and why, opening up the process to the group as much as possible, responding to ideas and suggestions, and remembering that this piece belongs to the group, you will be able to help them shape the theatre piece into a performance piece.

Spend some time preparing for and planning this change in role, both for yourself and the group.

(a) For Yourself

One of the main anxieties for you as a facilitator becoming a director may be what directing will demand of you.

Time:	10 minutes
Aim:	To consider the differences between your role as facilitator and as director.

DIRECTIONS:

Brainstorm the role for yourself: how do you think it differs from that of facilitator? In what ways might they clash? In what ways are they similar? What are your concerns about directing? Are there ways you can think of to address these (e.g. talk to someone more experienced, or read some of the resource material)?

Prepare a list of questions that you can refer to when you are watching a rehearsal, such as: are the characters' motivations clear? Are the relationships between characters clear? Is the piece interesting to watch? Is it varied in tone and pace? Can you hear and see the actors? What are they doing when they are not in a scene.

Simply spending some time considering these issues will prepare you for the changes.

(b) With the Group

Time:	20 minutes
Aim:	For the group to consider the role of the director.

DIRECTIONS:

Divide the group into three smaller groups and ask them to address these questions:

- What does a director do?
- How can the director support them as a group?
- How can they support the director?

Ask each group to feedback to the main group, and list what they have said on a flipchart.

Ask if anyone has anything to add to what has been said.

NOTE:

You may wish to refer to the groundrules (Unit One), as there will be many correlating points. However, don't be too anxious about the directing role – it is mostly a matter of common sense, and the more you watch rehearsals the more you will be able to offer!

Use this exercise in conjunction with the next one.

2. Rehearsal Preparation

Time: 30 minutes

Aim: To prepare the group for the transition from
                     devising to rehearsal, and the rehearsal process.

DIRECTIONS:

Divide the group into three smaller groups and ask the groups to brainstorm one of these questions each:

- What differences do they think there will be between the devising and rehearsing processes?

- What do they need to do now, in preparation for the show, in order to reach performance level?

- What qualities will they need to bring to rehearsals?

Feed these back to the main group, and add as appropriate. If necessary, refer again to the groundrules about concentration, support for each other and timekeeping.

Consider with the group what the fundamental aspects of rehearsal are (e.g. learning lines; knowing the running order; going over things several times; being flexible and changing things around).

Go through some basic theatre terms with them:

- 'Blocking' means the actions and moves that each character makes when on stage, as well as when one actor blocks someone else from the audience's view.

- A 'dress rehearsal' is the final rehearsal of the piece before the first performance, with all costumes and props (and lights in a theatre).

- 'Warm-ups' are the same as they have been doing, done every morning before rehearsals and before each performance.

- 'The call' is the time that they are required to be at the pick-up point (or at the theatre).

- 'Downstage' means the stage area nearest to the audience; 'upstage' means the area furthest from the audience.

- 'Wings' are the areas to the side of the playing area, often defined with curtains in a theatre.

Point out that there is no stage manager, and so they are responsible for their own props and costumes, putting them where they need to be and collecting them at the end of each show.

Agree a rehearsal schedule if you are using one, and when the dress rehearsal will be. Agree a date when all lines will be learnt, and when costumes are to be brought in, and where they will be stored.

3. Warm-Ups

Physical warm-ups and exercises for concentration are essential before rehearsals and performances, to warm up the body and voice in order to prevent strain, and to bring the group together before they perform. Different group members should lead the warm-ups, taking it in turns.

Encourage individuals to take personal responsibility for warming up, whilst also offering group exercises. You can refer again to the earlier games section, or use other exercises. For physical warm-ups *see* Tag Games, Unit One; Physical and Vocal Warm-Ups, States of Tension, Unit Two. For mental warm-ups *see* Concentration Games, Cooperation Games, Unit One.

Rehearsal Schedule

In a theatre production, there would normally be a schedule of rehearsals, where different sections are run at different times. This enables the director and cast to concentrate on separate scenes or sections, and means that not everyone has to be there all the time. If you have time to do this, it might be useful to draw one up – people can use their 'spare' time to learn lines individually or meet separately to go through scenes. It is not, however, time off and the group should be encouraged to think of all the rehearsal period as time for them to work on their scenes and take responsibility for using it effectively.

At Leap, we allow roughly one to one and a half weeks for rehearsals on a ten-week project. Once the group has started devising, the honing down process can become part of the rehearsal process, as they start to learn their lines, and remember what they are doing in each scene.

1. Sections

After rehearsing separate scenes, and once the running order has been agreed, it is useful to divide the piece into three or four sections that can be rehearsed as blocks of work. This helps break down the rehearsal process, practises the links between scenes, and helps people remember the running order.

So, for example, the first four scenes could constitute Section One, which you would run through, then give notes (see below) and then run through again before moving on to a different section.

2. Run-Throughs

As the first performance approaches, you will want to start doing regular run-throughs of the whole piece, so that all of you get a sense of how the whole piece works. As the director, run-throughs also offer you the opportunity to ask some vital questions:

- Does the pace vary enough – do some scenes speed up too much, and do others slow down?
- How do the scenes link together?
- What are the actors doing between scenes?

Start timing these run-throughs to see how long the piece is, remembering that you are aiming for around 40–45 minutes. If the piece is running at 50 minutes or more, you will probably need to go back over the scenes and check that they are running at no more than three minutes, and then cut them down where appropriate. You will usually find that there are up to five minutes that can be cut down simply through people remembering their lines and cues and getting the pace right so that it is not dragging.

Keep a record of the timing of the piece, and feedback during the notes session, encouraging them to lose some of the extra time.

3. Rehearsal Strategies

There are various strategies you can employ in rehearsals, that help focus on different areas, as well as relieving the boredom of doing a scene over and over again.

(a) Line Run

The line run is a very useful way of rehearsing without running a rehearsal. It can be done sitting down, and focuses the group's attention on what the actual lines of a scene are. Devising material sometimes glosses over hitches in the lines, and a line run can highlight a point where no line has actually been worked out or memorised.

The line run can also be used between full rehearsals, on individual scenes, and as a focusing exercise on the way to a performance. Ideally, the cast should be able to reel off their lines as quickly as possible.

(b) Speed Run

A line run can be run as a speed run where everyone says their lines as quickly as possible.

A rehearsal can also be done at top speed (excluding songs and moves), and doubles as a concentration exercise and as an energiser. The key is not to worry about the acting.

(c) Singing Run

This time the group sing their lines all the way through the rehearsal, exaggerating the emotions so that it seems like an over-the-top opera. Again, the emphasis here is not on acting, but on learning lines and becoming aware of shifts of emotion within the piece, as well as offering a fun way of relieving the monotony of rehearsals.

(d) What Are You Thinking?

This is an acting exercise, ensuring that each actor knows what they are thinking at a given moment, so that they can make full sense of their lines. As the actors run through a scene, call 'Stop!' Everyone freezes where they are in the scene, and you ask different characters what they are thinking at this point in the scene. This will help them clarify their thought processes. When you are satisfied that they know what they are thinking, the scene can continue where it left off.

Giving Notes

As the director, one of your most important tasks is to give feedback or notes following each rehearsal, a process followed in professional theatre. Make sure that you have a notebook and pen handy while you are watching, so that you can jot things down immediately. Things to look for might include:

- *Acting*: If a character's motivation or relationship isn't clear.

- *Presentation*: If you can't hear someone, or if someone is hidden from the audience's view.

- *Blocking*: If someone isn't moving as their character would, or they have no particular moves worked out for a scene, or if new blocking is required.

- *Lines*: If someone hasn't learnt or remembered their lines.

- *Affirmation*: Affirming when good work has been done, or a particular effort has been made.

Starting from the first rehearsal, after each run-through of the section or whole piece, gather the group round for notes. This will become a ritual that they expect and rely on, offering them the chance to hear some feedback and work on the piece accordingly. Start at the beginning of the piece and work through to the end, making sure that everyone is concentrating and listening all the way through. At first, some participants may find it difficult to hear 'criticism', as they may interpret it. Try and continue in the same vein as the devising process, being positive and affirmative, whilst being clear about what needs attention, and firm if something is not working or lines have not been learnt. Some notes will be for the whole group and some will be for individuals, but if people are not being directly addressed they can still listen – they might learn some useful tips. Dissuade individuals from offering their opinions on what someone should or shouldn't do, or criticising another participant for not learning their lines or getting something wrong. If everyone offers their opinions at this stage, it makes the notes session very long and unfocused. If someone wants to raise an issue that they think needs addressing, ask them to do so at an appropriate moment, perhaps after the notes session, or when you go through the notes for that particular section of the piece. If something arises that needs trying a different way, make time to do this, either straight after that notes session, or by giving a rehearsal call to allow time to go over that sequence.

The notes are a way of continuing to structure the piece, but are, inevitably, more directorial. Reassure the group that this is your role at this stage in the process, and that it does not mean that the piece has become yours. It is still their work, and you are supporting them by giving them the feedback to refine it and make it as good as possible.

Dress Rehearsal

At last you are reaching the point of actually having to perform in front of an audience. This is an exciting and challenging time for the group and the culmination of all their work. The dress rehearsal is the chance for them to run through the piece as if it were a performance but without an audience – or, rather, with you, the director, as the audience. Emphasise that everything must be set up and ready *as if it were a performance.*

Dress Rehearsal Check-list

- Set the date and time of the dress rehearsal.
- Run through the list of props, and ensure that anything that is not already on site will be brought in.
- Run through the list of costumes and make sure everyone understands they will be expected to wear them for the dress rehearsal.
- All lines to be learnt, as there will be no prompting.
- Everyone should know the running order.
- Everyone should know their exits and entrances.
- Be clear that there is to be no stopping or laughing if someone forgets a line or gets something wrong. They *must* go on with the

performance, and continue as they would if there were an audience there.

- Time the performance.
- Give notes afterwards.
- Practise the bow at the end of the show.

This means that the group will have to take responsibility for their own props and costumes, and know where they are set and when they will be used, and to change into their clothes ready for the dress rehearsal. This is a good time to get the group to think about what they will do if things go wrong; they cannot laugh or ask for a prompt, so they will need to be ready to think quickly and maybe improvise a couple of lines, or adapt the scene slightly, which also means that they will have to give their full concentration, all the way through, and not just when they are on stage themselves.

It means them completing the change from participants to performers, and aiming for the best standard they can set themselves.

Post Dress Rehearsal Notes

The dress rehearsal is notorious for going badly, and there is a saying that a bad dress rehearsal means a good performance. It is certainly true that people's anxieties may prevent them from giving their best at this stage, but don't despair; having a real live audience is an enormous boost, and you will inevitably find that the actual first performance is much better than you would have expected when you watched the dress rehearsal!

What this means is that notes after the dress rehearsal need to be done sensitively, as you do not want to induce a crisis of confidence at a time when most of the cast will be feeling very nervous. Use this notes session to reassure them that the show works very well, and if you have any criticisms try and keep them minimal and balanced with strong affirmations. Obviously, any last minute changes should be small ones, if there are any at all.

Above all, you want them to believe in themselves and their abilities, so use the time to build their confidence rather than dwell on mistakes.

PRESENTATION

The style of presentation employed by Leap relies on the group members to make the theatre piece visually exciting, dynamic and engaging for its audience. We aim to illustrate that creating theatre is an opportunity for all of us with or without access to extensive costumes and props. Our only set is a brightly painted canvas backdrop (foldaway), attached to poles which sit in

Figure 3.6 The backdrop

buckets of cement. This defines the acting area and helps to take the audience out of their usual youth setting and into an imagined world. We have also used a few chairs and stepladders on a number of occasions, to provide different levels on the stage.

The three main characters have one clothing accessory each, which clearly identifies who they are. This may be a hat, a scarf or a bag and the actor playing the character removes this when they are playing a different character in the group scenes. The whole cast wears neutral clothing, with different coloured T-shirts and dark jogging bottoms or jeans and additional accessories for different character parts, if necessary. If a group member shows a particular interest in costumes, this is a good opportunity to introduce them to the world of Wardrobe, without demanding too much. It is also an opportunity if you feel that someone has less to do in the play (although you should try to ensure that this does not happen) to give them a task which they are individually responsible for. Guide them in making a list of all the characters and deciding what their signifying accessories should be. Then, set them the task of compiling these items in consultation with the other group members, ready for the dress rehearsal.

THE WORKSHOP

The workshop is a crucial part of the tour 'package' and it is recommended always to offer a workshop with the performance, despite some venues' interest in the show on its own. The workshop:

- explores further the issues that are raised in the performance
- provides an interactive learning process for the audience
- engages the actors and the audience in a shared experience
- builds the actors' skills and experience of working with young people.

In Unit Two we spent some time developing the workshop leadership skills of the group. As well as this focused training period, it is important to have offered opportunities for group members to run games and exercises throughout the training and devising period, and for yourself and other group members to offer constructive feedback on their technique.

Experience and confidence is of substantial importance in workshop leading and this practice alone will serve to improve their facilitation skills greatly.

Also, the evaluation and reflection that you incorporate into the games and exercises that you run, as well as maximising the group's learning as participants, will foster a greater sense of their understanding of the workshop process. This will be reflected when they are facilitating.

1. Devising the Workshop

Time:	One hour, 45 minutes
Materials:	Flipchart paper, pens
Aim:	To devise a one-hour workshop to accompany the show and explore the issues.

DIRECTIONS:
Stage One: (15 minutes)
Refer to your earlier brainstorms of:

(a) aims of a workshop

(b) theatre techniques you have learnt

(c) the issues you want to explore in the piece.

Allow the group some time to review these brainstorms and to add any new ideas that they have at this later stage in the process.

Stage Two: (15 minutes)
Offer the group a template of a workshop outline (*see* The Facilitator's Guide) for them to work from and go through it. This will be a helpful base for the group, ensuring that the workshop has structure whilst also allowing for their creativity and input.

An example template could be:

(a) Hotseat the main characters

(b) Large group game (opening)

(c) Smaller group work (main body of work including brainstorming, image work, developing scenes)

(d) Sharing scenes plus feedback

(e) Large group game (closing and reflection).

Depending on how capable your group are, you could offer them more detail than this outline, with suggestions for games, themes for the brainstorm etc.

Stage Three: (30 minutes)
Divide the group into three or four smaller groups and ask them to add the detail to the workshop, with times allocated for each section, totalling an hour. Go around the groups and listen in and offer advice if they are struggling.

Stage Four: (45 minutes)
Get a spokesperson from each group to read out their workshop plan. As a whole group ask questions on how ideas would work, check that the timing is realistic, and challenge any parts that you feel would be unsuitable (if any), offering honest reasons why and affirming them for taking risks. As a group, decide whether you want to draw the best parts out of each workshop plan and create one, or whether you want to try them all out over the course of the tour.

Whatever your decision, make sure everyone understands how the workshop(s) will be run and has a written copy of the plan to refer to.

2. Hotseating: (see also Hotseating, Unit Three)

Time:	One hour
Aim:	To practise the hotseating and the role of hotseat facilitation.

DIRECTIONS:
The group will have experienced hotseating in the character development stage of the devising period, so the concept should not be completely new to them. Share the following guidelines for hotseating (which we use at Leap) with the group:

(a) The characters stay in character fully throughout the hotseating.

(b) The characters speak in the first person from their fictional experience, rather than making universal statements.

(c) The actors bear in mind their responsibility as 'educators' in answering the questions and do not give false information.

(d) There is a facilitator to facilitate the hotseating.

(e) The facilitator introduces the 'characters' to the audience at the beginning of the hotseating.

(f) The facilitator has a few prepared questions to ask the characters to start the process, if necessary, for example, 'I'd like to ask all three characters what their next step is going to be'.

(g) The facilitator fields any questions that are about the actors and the play, rather than the characters, for example, 'That's a great question, if you'd like to save it until the end when there will be a chance to find out about how we made the play'.

(h) The facilitator introduces the actors to the audience at the end of the hotseating.

Decide on which characters are going to be hotseated. It may be that you stick with the three main characters, or you may decide to hotseat more. Make sure that your decision balances the learning needs of your group with the audience's needs.

Practise the hotseating, with group members taking it in turns to facilitate, with the rest of the group asking the questions. Offer feedback on how they managed the eight aspects of hotseating above.

3. Leadership Skills (see also: Co-Leading, Unit Two)

Time:	10 minutes
Materials:	Flipchart, pen
Aims:	To identify the qualities and skills of a workshop leader.

DIRECTIONS:

Brainstorm all the skills and qualities of a workshop leader.

From the list, identify five key skills which group members can refer to when running the workshop. For example:

(a) give clear instructions

(b) support your co-workers

(c) make eye contact with the group

(d) be energetic

(e) ask open questions.

FEEDBACK AND DISCUSSION:

You may wish to deepen this discussion, and to spend some time discussing each skill. How can you support your co-workers? What happens if you have no energy? Why and how can you ask open questions? How does eye contact impact on the workshop?

4. Working Teams

You need to establish working teams for the workshop, and decide who is going to facilitate the hotseating, the first group game, the smaller groups, the sharing of scenes and the closing exercise. It is important that you allocate the teams yourself, rather than leaving it to the group to decide. This will avoid upset and ensure that the teams are not based on friendship groups but are selected to meet both the learning needs of the group members and the needs of the workshop participants. Make sure that:

(a) each smaller group has a strong worker

(b) the strengths and weaknesses of co-workers complement each other

(c) a confident and skilled group member facilitates the hotseating (at least for the first few workshops)

(d) the teams are mixed in terms of gender and race, if possible.

Reassure the group that you will be changing the teams around and that everyone should get a chance to lead different parts of the workshop. At Leap we change the teams around after three of four workshops. This gives the teams enough time to develop their co-working relationship but also gives everyone the opportunity to practise their skills at running different sections.

If you have a large group, not everyone will be needed at all times during the workshop and you will want to decide whether everyone should join in the games as participants if they are not leading them, or sit quietly at the side. This will vary for each workshop, depending on the numbers and the confidence of the participants, but it is good to establish some guidelines in advance.

Your performance piece is now ready for a public viewing, and your workshop is planned and facilitation roles allocated. All the pieces of the jigsaw should be in place – onstage and off – including the external organisation of the tour (*see also* Practicalities). On to the show!

UNIT FOUR

THE LEAP

During *the leap* itself, we are suspended in mid air, feeling nervous and exhilarated, yet with energy and power in our flight. We are in the midst of the experience, not sure of what the impact of the leap will be on ourselves or on the people around us, but knowing that the inevitable movement of the leap will propel us forward to our landing.

Unit Four: The Tour

UNIT GUIDE

Introduction
The Show and Notes
Preparation for the Tour
Continued Training and Group Cohesion
The Speak Out

INTRODUCTION

The tour is the point at which the group must step outside their 'comfort zone'. They have been working in a safe atmosphere of affirmation, trust and support and this experience must now operate as their backbone, providing them with the strength necessary to face the sometimes harsher criticism of their peers. They must support each other throughout the tour and you must keep building their confidence when they need it, as well as challenging their work when it falters. The theatre piece is their achievement and they have a right to be proud of it. They also have a responsibility to themselves and to the young people they are performing to, to focus their energy and be the best they can be – they are now 'peer educators'.

This is their voice, their stories, their experiences and their vision being shared with the wider community. It is their opportunity to be heard.

Whether you have been working together for three days, three weeks or three months, the first performance is an important benchmark in the project. Through the show (and the subsequent workshop), the participants will now communicate their experiences and concerns to a wider audience, and this is the real culmination of all their work.

Your role has changed to include that of a director, and they are now not only group participants, but a 'company' preparing for performance; we have used this term interchangeably with 'group' in this section to reflect this dual role.

THE SHOW AND NOTES
The Preview

After the dress rehearsal and before the first performance proper, you may find it helpful to do a preview of the show. This could take place at your centre, perhaps for a small group of workers – the audience should be a supportive one, who are ready to applaud. This can be a great opportunity to get some last minute feedback on the show, as well as giving the actors a chance to see how the piece works with an audience before being thrown to the lions in a youth club!

A different kind of preview could also be held for an invited audience of funders or people working in the field, perhaps those who may not get a chance to see the piece once it is taking place in a school or youth club. Obviously the stakes will be higher for this kind of preview, and you should make sure the cast are well prepared and rehearsed. Ensure that the audience knows they are attending a preview performance, and that it may not be perfect!

The First Performance

Now the company are ready to do their first performance for a group of young people in a venue. A check-list of important points follows.

1. Actors' Call

For the first show, it is advisable to call the actors to the centre well in advance of the time you need to leave for the performance. This leaves some leeway for people being late, or any last minute shopping for props, as well as time for a warm-up together.

Do a check-in, so that people can express how they are feeling (nervous!).

2. Warm-Up

It is essential to have a warm-up for the whole company, so that their voices and bodies are stretched, and the group is brought together as a unit.

This should include:

(a) Physical warm-up

(b) Vocal warm-up

(c) Group cooperation/communication warm-up

The whole warm-up does not need to take longer than 15 minutes. (*see also* Unit Two and Unit Three for examples of warm-up exercises.)

3. Load the Van and Go to the Performance Venue

Encourage all the group to take responsibility for loading and unloading the van, and try to ensure that it does not always get left to the same members of the group.

Figure 4.1 Unloading the van

4. At the Performance Venue

- Liaise with the staff at the venue, letting them know you have arrived
- Decide where in the venue you are going to perform
- Change into any costume, and stow bags and coats in a suitable storage place, perhaps with the venue staff
- Ask the company to walk around the performance space for a few minutes, getting a sense of how big it is, and to try out a couple of lines to hear the acoustics in the space. Will they need to speak up? Is there an echo?
- When it is close to performance time, bring the group together in the space, and do a quick exercise to raise their energy and awareness of each other.

5. Pre-Performance Energiser

At this point, you will want to do an exercise that is quick, raises energy, brings the group together and is fun. There are several exercises you could use, including call and echo sound and movement games; passing a rhythm or a phrase games (e.g. Zip Zap Boing); or a tag-type game: it will depend on the venue, how much space there is, and whether you have a group of teenagers watching you or not! Different people can lead this at different times, but you will probably want to support the group at their first show. Example exercises follow.

(a) Where's Maria?

Time:	5–10 minutes
Aims:	To raise energy and focus the group just prior to a performance (or rehearsal or training day).

DIRECTIONS:

This is a call and response game, for which the group stands in a circle. The calls and responses are as follows, some of which are a rhythmic stamp. Go through these one by one, then start stringing them together in a rhythmic pattern.

(i) You stamp your feet in this rhythm:

Ta ta ta ta

To which the response from the group stamping their feet is:

Tate tate tate ta.

(ii) This can also be reversed, so you stamp the rhythm:

Tate tate tate ta

And they respond:

Ta ta ta ta.

(iii) You say: 'Where's Maria?'

The group responds: 'I don't know'

You can repeat this a couple of times.

(iv) You say: 'Just relax'

The group responds by sighing loudly and sinking towards the floor.

NOTE:

This is reputedly a chant from Latin America, and the idea is to build up the different calls and responses into a variable rhythmic pattern. You can add your own calls and responses if you wish, but try and keep to the rhythm that has been established.

(b) Ball of Energy

Time:	3 minutes
Aim:	To raise energy and focus the group just prior to the show.

DIRECTIONS:

Ask the group to huddle round in a tight circle. Tell them to imagine you have a ball of energy, fizzing away in the middle, and they should all touch it to feel the energy. They all put their hands in the middle of the circle, moving them around and feeling the energy starting to move into their bodies. Very quickly, fire questions, such as 'What colour is it? What does it taste like? What does it smell like?' etc. which anyone can respond to, in any order, then tell them to start taking the energy in through their hands, arms, into their bodies, down into their legs and feet, till they are fizzing with that energy.

End with a jump in the air and a yell – and wish them luck!

6. Prepare for the Performance

Arrange with the company that you will introduce the piece and then give them the signal to start. As the audience start to take their seats, the cast should take their places in the performance space, ready to start. There should be no talking, and they can use these last few minutes to concentrate their minds on the coming performance.

7. Introduction

Once all the audience are seated and ready, do an introduction to give the audience a little background information:

- The company's name, how long they have been working together, and the purpose of the project.
- The title of the piece and how long the show lasts, mentioning that it has been devised by the group from their own experiences and their research.
- Mention that there will be a workshop afterwards, and that the audience will have a chance to ask the characters some questions if they want.
- Give the company the signal to start.

Make sure that you watch all the show and take some notes. Keep your attention focused on the show, and let the venue staff deal with any unruly audience members.

Figure 4.2 Introducing the show

Post-Show Notes (see also Giving Notes, Unit Three)

After the show and workshop, bring everyone back together, preferably back at your centre. This is a chance for them to reflect on the show, both individually and as a whole group.

After the first show, try and keep notes to a minimum, and once the show is up and running start reducing the number of times you give notes, so that it is not after every performance but perhaps every third show or so. These notes might centre on a drop in pace or movements or lines that are getting sloppy that need picking up on, or rediscovering the motivation behind a movement.

As the tour continues, keep an eye on the group and make sure that they continue to push to do their best at each performance – remind them of their aims, what they are trying to say, and the fact that each audience will be seeing the show for the first time.

(see also Continued Training and Group Cohesion, Unit Four.)

The Public Performance

Towards the end of the tour, it is great to do a public performance for family and friends, ideally in a theatre space. This need only be one night in a fringe theatre, or a studio space, but it should preferably have lights, so that the company feel that they are doing a 'real' show, which is very exciting for them and validates their experience. It is also another opportunity to invite any funders or workers or other interested parties who have not had a chance to see the show yet.

After the show, you could give an example of the hotseating session, allowing the audience to ask questions, but bear in mind that they will probably ask different questions than a youth club audience would.

We normally make a small charge for tickets in the venue – this not only helps pay for the hire of the theatre, but also makes the performance seem more professional and worth watching. You could also ask someone to design a poster for it, which the group members could hand round to friends, or keep for posterity!

Post-Workshop Notes (see also The Workshop, Unit Three)

As with the show, it is important to offer feedback to the group on the workshop, to continue their learning curve and to ensure that the quality of the workshop improves as they gain more experience and confidence. Set aside time back at your base for the whole group and for the smaller teams to evaluate the success of the workshop. You could use a go-round technique to share how each person found the workshop, or pose a focused question to discuss. For example: did they accomplish their aims? How was their relationship with the participants? Did they support each other? Get them to identify things they did well and things which could be improved.

Also, you may wish to observe a different team at each workshop and then spend some focused time with them alone feeding back on their style, support, etc.

It is good to have a 'go-round' after each workshop to allow the group to voice their feelings and concerns. You could also make post-workshop notes a regular feature of the weekly evaluation (see also Continued Training and Group Cohesion, Unit Four), perhaps focusing on a particular aspect of the workshop.

Suggestions for this subject include:

- Identifying and responding to the needs of different venue participants (e.g. schools or homeless hostels)
- The benefits and disadvantages of peer-led workshop
- How to deepen the learning of the workshop participants.

Figure 4.3 Running a workshop

PREPARATION FOR THE TOUR (see also PRACTICALITIES)

Preparation for you: you will need to be thinking about a lot of things at this stage of the project and good administrative support will be vital. Here are some things that will help the tour run smoothly.

1. Timing: giving yourself enough time is essential to avoid stressful journeys in traffic and late arrivals at the venue

   - Go through each venue in advance, working out an approximate drive time (be generous)
   - Give a call time that allows people to be late.

2. If you can share the driving of the van with a colleague, this is preferable.

3. Photocopy street maps of where the venues are, with the actual venue highlighted. Details of parking possibilities are also useful.

4. Have a contact name at the venue, as well as the telephone number in case of emergencies.

Preparation for the group: this is likely to be the first time the group members have done a tour and it will be an exciting, exhausting and tension-filled experience for them. Preparation is vital in helping them feel more secure and confident during this stage of the project.

Here are a list of possible ways to prepare the group, in advance of the tour.

1. Brainstorm the different venues you are visiting, such as schools, youth clubs, homeless hostels, and identify the different characteristics of the venues and what to expect of the participants (including the unexpected).

2. Go through the tour schedule with the group, briefly discussing each venue and raising any specific concerns, such as numbers of participants, space restrictions, early mornings, etc.

3. Make sure all group members are clear about the call times and have their own copy of the tour schedule to refer to.

4. Discuss and decide on how you introduce yourselves, for example as volunteers, actors, unemployed, young people etc.

5. Discuss the behaviour that you expect of yourselves and will be expected of you in the venues, for example no smoking, no swearing.

6. Reflect on issues around appropriate boundaries between the group members and the young people in the venues, for example physical contact, disclosing personal information, exchanging telephone numbers. (*see also* Working with Young People, Unit Two).

CONTINUED TRAINING AND GROUP COHESION

Once the tour has started, the daily routine changes drastically. The group are no longer meeting every day (or every week, or whatever) at a set time, and undertaking training together, or devising the show. The group cohesion is therefore in danger of disintegrating, as they no longer have this structure to hold them together. A new structure needs to be created, that will keep the group as a cohesive whole.

Strategies for Keeping the Group Together

1. Check-Ins and Warm-Ups

Always arrange to meet before a performance with enough time to have a check-in (*see* Group Work, Unit One), and to do a warm-up with the group (*see* Physical and Vocal Warm-Ups, Unit Two).

These will continue the function of bonding the group and focusing them on the task in hand. You will also want to allow time for people to meet and have informal chats, before starting the organised warm-up, so you could arrange to have the building open from half an hour earlier than the actual call.

2. In the Van

If you are travelling in a van to get to performances, try and ensure that the group meets at the centre and then travels together to the venue. Obviously, if someone lives right next door to the venue, then there is no point in them meeting with you at the centre. However, it is then doubly important that there is a warm-up at the venue, to bring the group together and focus their energy and concentration.

Equally, after the show, it is tempting for people to go off separately. At Leap, we have found it beneficial if people can travel back to the centre together. This time in the van is often vital in terms of group bonding and informal feedback, where the first laughter is heard about something that happened during the show, or when tensions are first expressed. Ideally, the whole company should be there for this experience, to help keep them together as a unit. It also means it is not always the same people going back to the centre, and unloading the van all the time, which prevents future resentment.

Quality time in the van together sounds silly, but is actually very important – although you will probably curse the singing by the end of the tour!

3. Having a No Show Day

If you are performing over three or four weeks, keep one day free each week plus the weekends, although occasionally you may have a special event on a Saturday, for example a conference or a festival, which is worth doing. At Leap, this continues the four-day week structure we have set up during the first part of the project, and allows people to recharge their batteries and get all their necessary day-to-day tasks done. Touring is very tiring, especially for beginners, and the group will appreciate this relaxation time.

It also continues to allow you, the facilitator/director, a day for planning and reflection.

4. Having a Weekly Session for Evaluation and Training

Following on from this, it is also useful to keep one morning or afternoon session free each week, preferably near the end of the week (such as Thursday afternoons). Keep the groundrules on the wall of the training room, and refer to them if necessary.

The purposes of this weekly session are:

- to give a chance for people to try different things, such as running a different section of the workshop which they are not sure about, in a safe environment and with feedback

- to give any notes that are outstanding

- to rehearse any changes that need to be made in the show

- to give the group a chance to play games together again, and enjoy being with each other outside the discipline of the tour

- to continue to develop their performance and workshop skills

- to continue with the weekly evaluation.

All these strategies will help keep the group together, and this will show on stage in improved communication and mutual support.

Run this session in a structured way, for example:

- Games/Warm-up

- Notes/Feedback

- The weekly evaluation

- A training session, with exercises

- Closing.

(a) Games

You could try some games that you have not played since the beginning of the project, or give people the opportunity to run some new games.

(b) Notes/Feedback

- Make any announcements

- Go over any outstanding notes

- If necessary, rehearse any (small) changes in the show

- Look at different sections of the workshop, such as the hotseating and seeing whether the questions are being fielded appropriately, and whether the facilitators of that section have some prepared questions.

(c) Evaluation

Alongside the general evaluation of the week (*see also* Group Work, Unit Two; and Post-Workshop Notes, Unit Four), you could ask the group to reflect on the work, and their skills, to help them identify areas that need working on.

Ask them to work in three groups, each group answering one of the following and then feeding back to the whole group:

- Which performances worked well and why?
- Which workshops worked well and why?
- What did they find difficult and why?

This not only helps the group to improve their evaluation skills, but also helps you address the areas they feel they need help in.

(d) Training

Use this session to undertake work with the company that you feel needs developing, or that they have identified needs addressing. Examples might include:

- Physical work, to help people move less self-consciously on stage: aside from regular warm-ups, do some further physical theatre exercises, to encourage people to 'think' with their bodies, and express themselves physically
- Vocal exercises to help them project their voices, including singing games
- Additional workshop skills to help them work with groups, such as asking open-ended questions, and deepening responses to questions
- Improvisation and creativity games and exercises, to help with acting skills.

By keeping the group together and offering continued training, you will find that the group are still engaged with and interested in the project, and this will mean that they will be able to offer more in the performance and workshop.

(e) Closing

As you would do normally, either at the end of a training day, or at the end of a workshop, do a closing exercise to finish off (*see* Closings, Unit One). This is especially important if this is the end of the week, as you may not be meeting again for two or three days.

Another event that will help to keep the group working together towards a common goal, is the Speak Out.

Figure 4.4 Additional training

THE SPEAK OUT

At Leap, we have developed the Speak Out as an integral element of the tour. The Speak Out is primarily an opportunity for young people to voice their experiences and their opinions and suggestions. It also places their experiences and the project in a wider context, signifying the importance of the work and its potential impact on the community. It is an event to which the participants can invite other young people who have direct experience of the issue to come and have their say, as well as people they have spoken to during their research, workers in the field, and any other interested parties (even MPs), to hear them. It is a chance for all these people to come together and share their concerns and their experiences, and discuss strategies for the future, ensuring that young people are included in the decision-making process.

It should be planned for the end of the tour, certainly in the last week, to act as a focal point of the project, and you can invite the participants to write songs or poems to perform at the event, as well as asking two or three professionals to speak about the theme. The group can also perform the theatre piece, and perhaps do a short hotseating session afterwards. You may also want to invite the local press, which would raise the profile of the issue, as well as your organisation. At a Speak Out, voices are heard!

An event like this takes a certain amount of planning, and you will need to start thinking about it once the tour is up and running.

Venue

At Leap, we have held a Speak Out in the local Council Chambers, and at our centre, the latter being far more informal. We found that the Council Chambers were too intimidating for the participants to feel comfortable about sharing their experiences, although it had the benefit of giving more gravity to the situation. Therefore, we would recommend a more intimate venue, but remember it will probably need to be booked in advance.

Time and Date

As mentioned above, ideally the Speak Out should come towards the very end of the tour, to act as a focus and to allow time for planning. The overall timing of the event should be around two hours, and take place in the 'twilight hour' at the end of a working day, around 4 p.m. to 6 p.m. This means that workers can include it in their normal working day, and therefore make the time to attend.

Participants – The Group

Discuss with the group what and when the Speak Out is, and what its aims are. Do this in plenty of time, and ask if anyone would like to speak or perform a poem or song, or create a short performance piece. These can be about their own experiences, or their thoughts and reflections on the issue after their research and devising work.

Once people have committed themselves to preparing something, keep an eye on their progress, perhaps allowing time at the weekly training sessions for rehearsals.

If people don't actually want to perform something (or even if they do), this is a good opportunity for people to help with the planning, and get some administrative experience, telephoning, writing letters, and sending out invitations etc.

Ask two of the group to introduce the event, and each speaker, and to thank everyone for coming at the end of the day.

The Speak Out is an important part of the project, and it is part of the group's responsibility as participants to ensure that it is planned and carried out efficiently.

Speakers

Aim to have a range of speakers who have something they want to say about the issue. For example, you might have:

- a worker from a voluntary organisation working in the field
- a service user, such as a hostel resident, or perhaps one of your group members who has direct experience of the issue
- a worker from a statutory organisation working in the field
- an MP with a particular interest in that field, or your local MP, who might be interested in what your organisation is doing in the long term.

Be aware that people have busy schedules, so you will need to book them well in advance, especially if you are inviting an MP or local councillor. Ask each person to speak for about 5–10 minutes about their particular concerns and experiences, and what they think needs to happen in the future. Allow time in your timetable for questions for each speaker.

Pre-Planning

After you have contacted interested people, get a provisional list of about ten speakers and group members who are performing. From this, schedule the programme in terms of time and varying the content, following a speaker with a poem for example. Remember to ask the speakers if they require anything, such as flipcharts etc., and make sure these are in place on the day. Allow a refreshment break after the speakers, for tea and informal chatting, and then a slot for the performance.

Share the planning with the group and keep them updated on what is happening, making sure that they continue to share responsibility for the event.

Audience

Alongside your own group, you may wish to invite other service users, hostel residents, workers from other voluntary and statutory organisations, funders of your organisation and others you have come across in the course of your research – anyone who you think might be interested in attending. Depending on the size of the venue, aim for 50–100 people, so that people's questions get heard and it is not too intimidating an audience for those who are performing or speaking. Ask people to RSVP on their letters, so you can estimate numbers.

Press

As mentioned above, you could invite your local press, and also any representatives of magazines or publications specifically concerned with the issue (e.g. *The Big Issue* if the issue is homelessness). If they can give you editorial space or a review of the event, this helps to raise the profile of the work.

The Big Day

Check-list:

- enough seats
- flipcharts etc.
- tea, coffee, biscuits
- programme with list of speakers and their organisations, and performers' names, with enough copies for everyone attending
- table with flyers and publications, and leaflets about your work.

If you like, you could have a smaller number of speakers, and get the audience into working groups to discuss strategies which they would then feedback to the whole group. These could be listed and sent to relevant MPs or local councils.

Figure 4.5 The Speak Out

The tour demands a constant renewal of energy, especially to cope with the difficult venues that you will be faced with. However well planned your tour schedule is (and this is a priority), there will still be times when things don't go smoothly. The phrase 'expect the unexpected' is a useful tool to accompany you on your way. Sometimes there will only be a small audience, or the traffic will be terrible and you will arrive late, or someone in the company will be sick or have personal problems that are getting in the way, or they will leave their costumes behind – the list of potential problems is endless. However, there is also an endless list of great rewards that you will experience with the company, including the first performance, their excitement and pride in their work, the positive feedback they will get, the laughter in the van, the funny moments on stage.

When the tour comes to an end, you will feel tired and relieved. After all that hard work, you now need to look back and evaluate, not only the tour, but the whole project.

UNIT FIVE

THE LANDING

At the end of *the leap*, we land in a new place, a different place to where we jumped from. Now we have the chance to look back to where we have come from, see the distance we've come and congratulate ourselves on our achievements.

Unit Five: Evaluation

UNIT GUIDE

Introduction
Purposes of Evaluation
Evaluation Methods
Other Forms of Evaluation
Example of Evaluation Form

INTRODUCTION

The project is now drawing to a close. The group have undertaken the training, they have applied their skills to devising a show and workshop, and they have performed the piece and run the workshop with various groups in various settings. They are in a different place to where they set out from, with new skills and experiences. They now need to look back at where they've come from, and see how far they've come and what changes they've made – to reflect on their experiences, and evaluate what they have learnt and achieved.

The evaluation is another vital element of the process – without evaluation and analysis there is no real learning, and no awareness of transformation. Evaluation consolidates what has been learnt.

There may also be anxieties and fears at the end of the project, especially if the group have worked together for a long time. People may be wondering what they will do next, and how they will manage the next step in their lives without the support of the group and the structure and routine of the project. Some of these questions can be addressed individually (*see also* Guidance and Support, Unit Seven), but the reflection process can also support participants as they make the transition to the end of the work.

At Leap, at the end of the project, we schedule an evaluation session: this should be a whole day, if it is a full-time project, or a whole session for a weekly project. We use various methods to evaluate, as we find using different approaches to considering the work can offer new insights. You can mix and match from the following exercises, as appropriate to your group. We would recommend that you do at least one exercise each as individuals or pairs, as small groups and as a whole group. The evaluation process is also useful for you as a facilitator and will help you plan your work for the future.

Evaluation is part of achievement: you may see some of the mistakes you made, and so now be able to learn from them – but you will also see your successes, and these can then be celebrated.

PURPOSES OF EVALUATION

Time:	30 minutes
Materials:	Paper, pens
Aim:	To consider the purposes of evaluation, in preparation for the evaluation process.

DIRECTIONS:

Explain to the group what the session is about, and that you are going to do some exercises in groups and individually.

Divide the group into three smaller groups, and ask each one to think about the purposes of evaluation, and list them.

These can then be fed back to the main group, and added to as appropriate. Some of the main reasons for evaluation are:

- to allow the participants to see their development and consolidate their learning
- to inform the facilitator's work
- to provide the background to future projects and assist in planning
- to convince funders, organisations, parents etc. of the ability of the organisation to deliver the work
- to provide concrete evidence of the value of the work.

VARIATIONS/DEVELOPMENT:

Brainstorm with the whole group what they will be evaluating in terms of their own development, identifying what they are assessing. Examples might include:

- Problem-solving skills
- Developing confidence
- Communication skills
- Physical skills, such as physical theatre
- Acting skills

- Workshop facilitation skills
- Group work/team work.

EVALUATION METHODS
1. Individual (see **Example of Evaluation Form, Unit Five**)
Probably the main traditional form of evaluation is the written questionnaire. This is a useful way of asking people to reflect individually on their own experiences. They can be anonymous if they wish, which means they can be honest.

Time:	Up to one hour
Materials:	Prepared questionnaires and pens for each member of the group

DIRECTIONS:

Ask people to sit separately, and not to confer while they are filling the questionnaires out. Give them enough time to fill out the forms without hurrying.

NOTES:

Include this evaluation in the time you have set aside, rather than allowing people to take the forms home to fill them out. They are much less likely to return them to you later, and their thoughts and feelings may not be as fresh. Reassure them that the forms will not be read until after the project has finished, and that you are genuinely interested in all their feedback, and would appreciate an honest evaluation.

2. Pairs

Time:	30 minutes
Aim:	For pairs to support and coach each other in evaluations

DIRECTIONS:

Ask the group to get into pairs and call themselves A and B. Give the whole group a question to think about. In each group, B then supports and coaches A in answering that question and they then swap over.

Example questions might be:

- In what way will you use the work undertaken on the project?
- What is the first thing you will do on Monday morning to make that happen?

- How will you support yourself when you are doing the work?
- What are your long-term aspirations for using this work?
- What are the first steps you will take towards this?

Give each pair time to make notes on what they have decided; B could do this for A, and vice versa.

FEEDBACK AND DISCUSSION:
Each pair is invited to feedback to the main group some of their answers to the questions.

VARIATIONS:
You could also use Images with pairs (*see below*: Small Groups).

3. Small Groups
(a) Images

Time:	About 30 minutes, depending on size of group
Aim:	To use still images to pinpoint moments of learning on the project, using physical rather than written work to offer a different insight into the learning.

DIRECTIONS:
Divide the group into smaller groups of four or five. Ask each group to create three images each:

- The best moment of the project
- The worst moment of the project
- The funniest moment of the project.

In order to do this, they will need to spend time discussing their individual responses to these questions, so give them about ten minutes to do this.

The images can then be a composite of all their answers, or they can select one as being the most representative that resonates for all of them.

FEEDBACK AND DISCUSSION:
When each group has got three images, share them with the rest of the group. Ask the other group members to guess what the images are referring to, and the group showing the images to explain, where necessary. You will probably find that some of the images overlap, offering a shared experience of those moments.

Figure 5.1 The best moment of the project

VARIATIONS:

This work could also be done in pairs. You could also select different moments of the course that you would like them to focus on, such as a moment of learning on the course, or the most memorable moment.

(b) Play in Three Minutes

Time:	30 minutes
Aim:	To use drama and physical work to sum up the project.

DIRECTIONS:

Divide the group into smaller groups of four or five. Ask each group to create a dramatic representation of the project, events and experiences, that must not last longer than three minutes. Give them ten minutes to do this. Encourage them to use different dramatic techniques and styles, and to be as humorous as they like!

FEEDBACK AND DISCUSSION:

Share the pieces with the whole group.

VARIATIONS:

This exercise is based on a game where each group shows a film in three minutes, so you could also use it in this context. (*see also* Games, Light and Livelies, Unit Two.)

4. Whole Group Work

(a) Smiles, Frowns and Lightbulbs

Time:	15–30 minutes
Materials:	Flipchart, pen
Aim:	For the whole group to assess the course together, using brainstorms.

DIRECTIONS:

Gather the whole group around the flipchart. On the flipchart, create three columns, headed Smiles, Frowns and Lightbulbs. Explain that you are going to ask them to call out aspects of the course that they thought were good or worked well (smiles); those that were bad or difficult (frowns); and moments of inspiration or learning (lightbulbs). It is important to mention that one person's smile is another person's frown or lightbulb, and vice versa, and that things can therefore appear in more than one column. Also, this is like an ordinary brainstorm in that there is no censoring, and everything is written down.

(b) Reassessing Hopes and Fears (see also Hopes and Fears, Unit One)

Time:	Up to one hour
Materials:	Hopes and fears sheets from the first session
Aim:	To look again at the hopes and fears recorded at the beginning of the project and compare with feelings now.

DIRECTIONS:

Pin the sheets up on the wall, allowing people time to look through them, and recall how they felt on the first day, and what they wrote down about their hopes and fears then.

FEEDBACK AND DISCUSSION:

Bring the group together in a circle and ask them to feedback on any comments they wish to make about what they felt then and what they feel now. Go round the circle and ask each person in turn. What were they afraid of? Did they overcome their fear? What did they hope to gain from the project? Did they do this? What else have they gained on the way? It is important that these responses are not analysed or commented on by the facilitator or group members, but heard and acknowledged.

VARIATIONS:

If you do not wish to set this up as an actual exercise, just pin the sheets up on the wall at the beginning of the day or session, and allow people to look at them informally and individually recall how they felt. This information can then be fed into another evaluation exercise, such as the written questionnaires, or the image work.

(c) *Written Affirmations*

Time:	Minimum of one hour
Materials:	One sheet of paper per group member, plus pens and pencils, all of which can be multi-coloured.
Aim:	For group members to affirm each other through anonymous written work.

DIRECTIONS:

Ask the group to sit in a circle, each with a sheet of paper and access to pens. Ask them to write their name at the top of the sheet, and then pass it to the next person. Then ask everyone to write an affirming statement about the person whose name appears on the sheet and then pass it on round the circle, so that everyone writes a sentence about every other member of the group. The affirmations should be about the person themselves, and not about the way they look – something that the person can take pride in having offered the group, or something they have learnt to do, or something they have overcome.

The statements are anonymous.

When everyone has finished the statements, return them to their owners, who should be given time to read through them.

FEEDBACK AND DISCUSSION:

Ask if anyone wants to read their sheet out, but do not force people if they do not want to. Ask the group to lay their sheets out on the floor for everyone to read the finished papers. Some people may not want to do this when the group are there, and may prefer to take them home to read them.

NOTES:

Some people find affirmation exercises extremely difficult to receive: if they have very low self-esteem, they may be overwhelmed by receiving so many positive comments, and may become tearful or try to belittle the comments, and they may try to hide or lose their sheets. You will need to continue the affirmation work, by encouraging people to trust the affirmations and believe what they say. They may enjoy reading them on their own at home.

(d) Circle Affirmations

Time:	30 minutes
Aim:	For the whole group to affirm each other directly.

DIRECTIONS:

Ask the group to stand in a circle. Going round the circle for each group member, ask for three affirmations about each person, to be spoken by three different people in the group at random. For example one person might say: 'I would like to thank … for his sense of humour and overcoming his fear of trust exercises'. The person says: 'thank you'.

Then two other people around the circle, but not in any particular order, would then add their affirmations, and the person thanks each of them.

Then you move on to the next group member in the circle, until everyone has received three affirmations.

NOTES:

Make sure different people offer the affirmations. Again, this exercise may be very difficult for some people to receive, and you need to be sure your group will be able to cope with it. It is quite challenging to receive affirmations face to face, and some people may actually become upset, or giggle or not be able to look up from the floor. However, this may be a challenge you think will be useful to them, so exercise your judgement accordingly.

Encourage them to write down what they have been told, while it is fresh in their minds, so that they will be able to refer to them. Reassure them that this is not 'conceited' or 'vain' or whatever words they are using. These statements have been made by people about them in a caring, positive environment, and of course they are going to want to remember them.

VARIATIONS:

A simpler form of this affirmation is for each person to step into the middle of the circle, for the facilitator to call out 'Let's hear it for …', and for the rest of the group to applaud them.

(e) A Party

Perhaps the most obvious way to end the project is by having some kind of party or celebration. This could be a traditional party with music and dancing, or you could perhaps have a communal meal.

OTHER FORMS OF EVALUATION

Other methods of evaluation are discussed in Practicalities, and include the facilitator's report and documentation and the venues' evaluations. You could also undertake individual progress reports throughout the project, where you could discuss their development with participants.

Other ways of assessing a project might include:

- monitoring acceptance on courses or employment of participants
- monitoring changes in the group itself, their interactions and attitude
- monitoring attendance figures over the project
- assessing participants' involvement in the decision making
- assessing improved academic performance
- other workers' evaluations
- collating statistics.

EXAMPLE OF EVALUATION FORM

Leap Theatre Workshop Post-Project Evaluation

(Please return to the Leap Theatre Workshop Project Manager. Thank you for filling it in.)

Name: *(leave blank if you want to stay anonymous)*

What first interested you in attending the introductory workshop?

After the workshop what encouraged you to join the project?

What was your biggest fear/concern with joining the project?

Was this overcome during the project? If so, how?

What were your expectations of the project and were they fulfilled?

What did you enjoy most during the training/devising period?

What did you enjoy least during the training/devising period?

What did you enjoy most during the touring period?

What did you enjoy least?

How did you find the style of the project leaders?

What skills/qualities do you feel you gained from this project?

What skills/qualities do you feel you contributed to the project?

What was your greatest moment of learning on the project?

How do you feel about the project ending? What are your plans?

Any suggestions for improvements?

This marks the end of the evaluation stage with the group. The next unit looks at some of the problems you may encounter along the way when undertaking this work.

UNIT SIX

STUMBLING

Things might not be as smooth as you hope either during the run-up or *the leap* itself. You might stumble, fall and hurt yourself and need support and help in getting back on your feet. Try to take the opportunity for learning that lies in the fall, rather than becoming stuck in the hurt and pain.

Unit Six: Confronting Conflict

UNIT GUIDE

Introduction
What is Conflict?
Strategies for Addressing Conflict
Conflict Scenarios
Moving on from Conflict

INTRODUCTION

Conflict is an inevitable part of life, and bringing together a group of vulnerable young people with different experiences, needs, backgrounds, ages, cultures and viewpoints is bound to lead to some conflict situations. These can arise between group members over differences of opinion, insensitive behaviour, miscommunication and misunderstanding, individuals not wanting to 'lose face' … the list is endless. You may experience a whole range of behaviours from group members, including sulking, shouting, avoiding, blaming or crying. Remember, you are working with young people who may have had unhealthy relationships, and may have already experienced hurt and rejection in their lives. Assumptions by group members and yourself about the experiences of others in the group can lead to people feeling threatened or unsafe. A good starting premise is 'don't assume anything'. As you gain more insight into the participants' lives, and they gain insight into each other's, you can learn what sparks individuals off, what types of exercises they always need to go to the toilet during (!), or what subjects they focus on repeatedly. This information will enable you to work sensitively with individuals and to gauge the intensity of work they are able to cope with.

The important thing is not that conflict exists, but how we deal with it. You may be tempted to ignore it and pretend it's not there or say to the group 'we have a performance to put on, let's just get on with it'. This is quite understandable; however, be honest – is this because of your own feelings of not knowing how to deal with the conflict? Most of us do not learn how to confront conflict in our lives, but the group process should not be sacrificed for the play, and the play should not be an excuse to avoid dealing with issues. There will be times when the play must be put first, and reminding the group of why they are all here is also a useful strategy to bring them together again. There are other skills and strategies that we can learn and draw on to help us resolve conflicts in the group. The group contract (*see* The Contract, Unit One) is your first strategy, providing the group with clear boundaries and an established process to deal with conflict when it arises. Also, the group work, weekly feedback and trust exercises are ways of uniting the group, creating a safe space to voice concerns and minimalising the likelihood of conflicts.

This chapter provides you with a closer look at what conflict is and some case studies of possible conflict situations, as well as a selection of strategies for you and the group to learn and practise during the training period of the project. If you feel this is not enough, you can always seek training for yourself in dealing with challenging behaviour and conflict resolution skills (*see* Resources). These skills will benefit you greatly throughout the project and no doubt throughout life!

At the core of this work is Leap's belief that conflict can be creative rather than destructive and that it provides an opportunity for growth and change.

WHAT IS CONFLICT?

You can prepare for conflict both with the group and by yourself, considering its causes and consequences, and responses to it.

Often our first reaction to the word is a negative one, but it is possible to move beyond that and find the positive aspects of conflict. The following two exercises should be undertaken early on in the project, so that you and the participants have considered the meaning of, and possibilities contained within, conflict before it actually arises.

1. Individual Alphabetical Brainstorm

As the facilitator, the group will turn to you when things are going 'wrong' and expect you to deal with the problem. We have outlined some strategies for both you and the group to use when addressing conflict (*see below*) but it would also be useful for you to consider your own response to the word.

Time:	10 minutes
Materials:	Pen, paper
Aim:	An individual exercise to explore the meanings of 'conflict'.

DIRECTIONS:

Write the word 'conflict' at the top of the piece of paper and then write the letters A through to Z. Brainstorm the word 'conflict' for yourself, writing at least one word for each of these letters (e.g. A – aggression; B – bad; C – change; etc. don't worry too much about X and Z!). Give yourself five minutes to do this, so that your responses are really quick.

If your responses are mostly negative, see if you can form a list of positive words, using the letters of the alphabet as above.

Ask yourself the following questions:

- What are your usual responses to situations of conflict?
- Are they always the same, or do they depend on the circumstances, or who the conflict is with?
- What feelings do you experience in conflict situations?
- What strategies do you already use to address conflict?
- What other positive aspects are there to conflict?

This preparation work will help support you and the group if and when situations of conflict arise, as you will have already considered them as a positive force for change.

2. Four Word Build (see also Group Work, Unit One)

Time:	30 minutes
Materials:	Pens, paper, flipchart
Aim:	A whole group communication/cooperation exercise, exploring the different meanings of 'conflict'.

DIRECTIONS:

Ask each participant to write down four words they associate with the word 'conflict'. Give them three minutes to do this. Next, each person finds a partner, and each pair shares their words. They then select a new combination of four words from their two lists, without adding any new words but ensuring that the new four-word combination is agreed by both of them. Keep a time limit of about five minutes on this section.

After this, the pair finds another pair, and they repeat the process, to create a new list of four words that they all agree on, composed of words from each pair's list. This four then hooks up with another four, and repeats the process, until the whole group are working together on creating a list of four words that they can all agree on that represent 'conflict'. Write these up on the flipchart.

FEEDBACK AND DISCUSSION:

Ask the group whether they are satisfied with this final list. Are all the words negative, or did they find some positive words as well? If they are all negative, can they now think of any positive words that might also be associated with conflict, for example the situation after a conflict has been resolved (e.g. growth, change, understanding, peace, unity etc). What are the aspects of conflict that lead to these positive outcomes? How did they feel when initially asked to consider conflict, and have these feelings changed through the exercise?

Then ask them to reflect on the process of creating this list: how difficult was it to compromise their ideas? How did they find ways to reach agreement? How useful might this method be for a group making decisions or reaching an agreement on something? What insight did it give them into conflict, how they normally behave in a conflict situation, and the feelings associated with it? Were there any positive outcomes to the exercise?

VARIATIONS/DEVELOPMENT:

This could be developed into a drama exercise: divide the group into four smaller groups, and ask each group to take one word and create an image of it. These images can then be brought to life (see also Image Work, Unit Two), or developed into scenes, continuing the theme of conflict.

NOTE:

This exercise could also be used with other words as a way of exploring an issue.

STRATEGIES FOR ADDRESSING CONFLICT

The other work you should undertake with your group is to offer training in strategies for addressing conflict that might differ from their normal responses. It is important in any conflict that all views are heard and acknowledged before moving towards some form of agreement, but many of us find it difficult to express ourselves assertively in a conflict situation.

Part One

These strategies offer some approaches with a view to creating a positive outcome, and will give your group a framework that they all know and understand, which they can then draw on should conflict arise. They are especially useful in preventing conflict or in the early stages of conflict.

1. Changing the Pattern

Time:	One and a half hours
Materials:	Flipchart, pens
Aim:	To explore aggressive and avoiding behaviours.

DIRECTIONS:

As a whole group brainstorm the words 'attack' and 'avoid', allowing two minutes for each word.

Now ask the group to brainstorm:

- Attacking or aggressive behaviour, body and verbal language
- Avoiding or defensive behaviour, body and verbal language.

Examples of aggressive behaviour might include shouting, criticising, interrupting, fighting, bullying; body language might include pointing, pushing, banging tables; vocabulary might include swearing, racist or sexist language.

Examples of avoiding behaviour might include sulking, laughing, feeling ill or depressed; body language might include folding arms and crossing legs, avoiding eye contact; and vocabulary might include apologies and hesitations.

Now ask the group to think of examples of why people behave in this way, for example: feeling angry but being polite, as 'women are not supposed to get angry'.

As a whole group, now brainstorm the word 'assertive', again allowing two minutes. Now ask them to brainstorm assertive behaviour, body language and vocabulary.

Examples might include: stating, negotiating, active listening, acknowledging, maintaining eye contact, using phrases like 'I think' or 'In my opinion'.

Now ask them to get into groups of three, and take an example of a situation of conflict in their own lives, with an aim they are trying to achieve. Each group then role plays the situation using each of the three different behaviours: attacking, avoiding, and assertive, in order to test the impact of each.

FEEDBACK AND DISCUSSION:

Ask each small group to share their role plays and ask the rest of the group to feedback on them.

What responses did each behaviour get? Which was the most effective in achieving the aim? Which behaviour did they find most natural and which most difficult? What effect might these new insights have on their own behaviour in future?

NOTE:

Make sure that you establish that these are patterns of behaviour and that they can therefore be changed: it is the behaviour not the person involved, and we all use different behaviour patterns at different times. This exercise will help participants identify their own and others' behaviour, and establish a framework for a different way of relating to others.

Figure 6.1 Attack and avoid

2. 'I' Statements

Time:	One hour
Materials:	Pen, paper
Aim:	To practise a strategy for making non-judgemental statements in an assertive way.

DIRECTIONS:

Following on from the previous exercise, introduce the idea of the 'I' statement, explaining that it is an example of asking for what you want in an assertive way, a way of expressing your view of a situation, how it is affecting you and how you would like to see it change. An 'I' statement should be as objective as possible, rather than carrying blame, and should allow room for discussion and negotiation. It should avoid being a 'You' statement as in 'You never do the washing up, you're really lazy and you need to pull your weight'. Rather, 'I' statements are a structured formula to address conflict in a non-judgemental way. Although they may seem awkward to use at first, they can also be adapted, using language people feel comfortable with, so that they have their own way of saying the statements. Once understood, they provide a useful common framework for the group.

Write up the 'I' statement formula on the flipchart:

- *When:* making the statement of fact in an objective way
- *I feel:* acknowledging the subjectivity of your emotions
- *What I'd like is:* stating the desired outcome, but without the expectation of change.

Introduce the idea to the group with an example of a situation where conflict might arise, such as a friend continually being late for meetings, then demonstrate an 'I' statement that could be made in that situation. For example:

When: you arrive late

I feel: anxious about you and uneasy about waiting on my own

What I'd like is: for us to agree a meeting time that suits us both.

or:

When: I come down in the morning and see dirty crockery by the sink

I feel: frustrated

What I'd like is: to organise a rota for washing up.

Get the group into pairs, and ask each person in each pair to consider a situation of conflict, perhaps relating to a current difficulty in their lives, with a friend, flatmate or partner, and then to formulate an 'I' statement to address it. The other person can then coach them, helping them make their 'I' statements clear, and you can also go round the pairs helping them with this where necessary.

Once they have formulated their 'I' statements, ask them to practise saying them to each other. This time the other person in the pair can look at the body language being used, with reference to the aggressive and avoiding behaviour lists above, as well as offering potential responses to the 'I' statement.

FEEDBACK AND DISCUSSION:
Bring the whole group back together and ask them to reflect on the process of making and saying their 'I' statements. How difficult was it to formulate them? Did they find it easy to say them, once they had formulated them, or did they find that their body language was saying something different to the words of the 'I' statement? What response did they get to their 'I' statements? How did

this compare to other responses they have received when raising these issues before?

NOTE:

Point out that these statements can be drawn on by the whole group if and when conflict arises within the group, giving them a mutual vocabulary that they can all use.

Ask them to try out their 'I' statements in the real situation in their lives, and try and agree a time for them to feedback to the group on how this went.

(*see also* Groundrules, Unit One.)

Part Two

The next few exercises offer you a selection of creative strategies for addressing a conflict situation once it has happened, when you feel intervention is necessary or it has been requested. Some are suitable for dealing with a whole group conflict, others are more appropriate for use when two or three people are in dispute. It is important that you consider their appropriateness to your given situation and use your own judgement as to their suitability.

1. Listening Exercise (see also Group Work, Unit One)

Time:	One hour
Materials:	An object to use as the 'speaking stick'
Aim:	To defuse a group conflict by encouraging group members to understand each other's views and to remove the tension and hostility that emerges when discussing a contentious issue.

DIRECTIONS:

Gather the group in a circle and explain that the reason for the gathering is to discuss the subject of the conflict in a structured and safe way. The rules of the discussion are as follows:

(a) You can only speak when you are holding the 'speaking stick'. When you have finished speaking, return the speaking stick to the centre of the circle.

(b) You must always summarise what you have just heard said by the person before you, prior to making your own point, for example 'what I heard you say is that you feel unhappy about me using that language as you find it insulting. I feel that ...'.

(c) Make your point concisely.

NOTES:

This exercise slows down the interaction between disputants and ensures that they listen to each other and take on board different points of view before expressing their own. It is a slow process, but is useful to prevent a situation getting over-heated.

VARIATIONS:

It can be used in a pair as well as a whole group.

2. Drama is Conflict

Drama is a great way to explore conflicts – after all most dramas are about conflict! You can use drama to express different points of view, to explore feelings associated with a situation, to problem solve and to discover more imaginative and creative resolutions.

(a) Look at it Both Ways!

Time:	One hour
Aim:	To reflect the situation back to the disputants, increasing their understanding and offering them the chance to see the incident from a different perspective.

DIRECTIONS:

(i) The first thing you need to assess is whether the conflict which has emerged is suitable to be brought to a forum like this. Here are some questions to help you decide:

- Are the disputants stuck in their positions?
- Can you pinpoint a main incident to focus the exercise on?
- Do you think the disputants will be able to work with their experience in this way without feeling too threatened or exposed?
- Do other group members know what is going on?
- Are the disputants willing to take part in this exercise to try to resolve the conflict?

If the answer to all these questions is yes, then continue with this exercise. If some of the answers are no, then you should try other strategies to address the situation.

(ii) Speak to each of the disputants (A and B) alone prior to this exercise for 5–10 minutes to give them the space to clarify their thoughts and to identify the incident that the exercise is to focus on.

(iii) Bring the group together and inform them that this exercise is to support A and B in resolving their dispute. Remind them that it takes a great deal of courage to bring this conflict into the arena and that the safety and trust of the group is paramount.

(iv) Ask A and B each to choose a group member to role play them in the exercise.

Give each of them five minutes alone with their role player, informing them of what has happened, what sparked the incident and what the outcome was from their point of view. Also, give each of the role players labels to wear with fictional names on, decided by A and B.

(v) Explain that the role play will be improvised and that although based on fact, it is now a fiction. The group must accept this (especially A and B) and look for the learning that there is to be had in the exercise. Also explain that at various points in the role play you will clap your hands and freeze the action and ask the actors questions to find out more about their thoughts and feelings. For example: 'Charlie, what are you thinking now?', 'Jenny, what did you feel when he said that?'

(vi) When you have set the exercise up fully, ask the role players to freeze in a starting position and then clap your hands to bring the role play to life. Bring the improvisation to a close, if it doesn't end naturally.

FEEDBACK AND DISCUSSION:

(i) Ask for audience comments about what they have just seen (excluding A and B). Stress that you are not wanting comments of blame and accusation, such as 'it was his fault', but any constructive insights into the problem: ideas, feelings they had and possible solutions they saw whilst watching.

(ii) Ask each of the role players, in role, for their feedback. How did they feel about the situation, what thoughts did they have? What would they like to say to the other character?

(iii) Ask each of the role players to take off their labels and to stick them on a chair, and welcome back the group member by giving them a round of applause (*see also* Deroling Techniques, Unit Two). Now invite them, out of role, to speak to the character they were playing (symbolised by the label on the chair) and to offer any advice, comments, and insights they had whilst playing them.

(iv) Finally, offer A and B five minutes each to feedback any learning they had from the exercise. Remind them that they are here because they want to resolve the dispute. Did they learn anything about themselves from the exercise? Did they gain new understanding about how the other is feeling, too? Did they see any new solutions?

How might they be able to move on?

VARIATIONS:

Rather than using other group members to role play the situation, ask A and B to role play each other (role reversal), to provide them with an insight into how the other person is feeling. This can be done with or without the rest of the group present.

DEVELOPMENTS:

Is there a second stage? Do the disputants now need to see possible solutions role played in order to move them on? If so, go on to Changing the Outcome.

(b) Changing the Outcome (see also The Forum Technique, Unit Two)

Time:	One and a half hours
Aim:	To explore solutions to a situation of conflict.

DIRECTIONS:

(i) Decide on a theme that underlies the situation of conflict currently being faced by members of the group, such as 'difference', 'power' or 'rejection', and construct a question that requires group members to think about the relevance of that theme to their lives, for example think of a time you were rejected, or think of a time you felt powerless.

(ii) Divide the group into smaller groups of three or four and pose the question to each group, asking them to share their personal responses to the question. Give each person two minutes to share their story and remind them not to disclose anything they do not want to share later with the whole group.

(iii) Ask each group to decide on one person's story which they can all identify with. Then ask the person whose original story it is to cast their group and build their story into a short scene. Give each group 15 minutes to devise the scene.

(iv) Share one of the scenes once through.

(v) Re-run it and invite audience members to stop the action and offer suggestions for alternative ways to resolve the situation. Encourage members to 'try out' their suggestions on stage. Your role as facilitator is to keep the exploration moving and to keep the dialogue going between the actors and the audience. Let the audience make the decisions about what point of the scene they want to replay the action from. Questions to ask the audience include: What was their strategy? Was it successful? If so, in what way? If not, why not?

(vi) Repeat steps (iv) and (v) with the other scenes.

FEEDBACK AND DISCUSSION:

What did the group learn from this exercise about their own situation? What is stopping them from trying out the most successful strategies?

NOTE:

This exercise is most suitable when those involved in the dispute have already had an opportunity to express their feelings and are ready to think about finding a way forward. You need to bear in mind whether the participants will be able to distance themselves enough from the immediate conflict situation to address it in this way.

(c) Mirror Mirror

> Time: One hour
>
> Aim: To use analogy to address sensitive issues.

DIRECTIONS:

(i) Before taking this exercise to the group, think about the situation of conflict that has arisen. Can you find a parallel situation, or analogy, that mirrors the real problem? Is there a myth, legend, fairy story or metaphor that you could use? Could you set the conflict in a different time or on a different planet? For example, if you have identified that there is a problem with two cliques emerging in the group and you want to address it, you could set up a dramatic activity based on two tribes, each with their own resources and set of rules, having to find a way of working together to survive.

(ii) Bring your idea for the drama to the group and set up the activity. You will need to know what the activity is, what you want to achieve and how you are going to set it up. Do you want them to work in smaller groups and share their pieces with each other? Do you want them to work as a whole group, then feedback on the experience?

FEEDBACK AND DISCUSSION:

Ask the group: Why do you think we did this exercise? Are there any parallels that you can identify between this drama and your own lives? What did the activity highlight for you? Did you have a point of learning from creating your own piece or from watching another group's piece? Do you have any new insights into the problem or possible ideas for resolving it?

3. Mediation (see also Three Ways of Listening Exercise, Unit One)

Mediation is a process in which a neutral third party intervenes in a dispute, not to decide on a course of action but to guide the disputants to a solution which is identified, chosen and agreed by themselves. It is increasingly being recognised as a successful route to the resolution of conflicts in which a win–win situation can be achieved for both parties as opposed to the more traditional win–lose style. The role of the mediator(s) is not that of judge and jury, but rather of one who builds trust, is impartial at all times and hands over control to those involved. Working with a co-mediator can be beneficial, allowing one person to listen actively and ask questions while the other takes notes. Mediation values and includes people's emotions in the process and provides a space for concerns and needs to be expressed and heard. It is a process of resolution much in line with the ethos of Leap's theatre making and as such commands inclusion in this book.

Time:	One and a half hours
Aim:	To resolve conflicts between disputants through an impartial mediator.

DIRECTIONS:

Suggest mediation as a possible way forward to the disputants, explaining what is involved, stressing that it is voluntary and that they have to want to resolve the situation. If both parties agree to give it a go, then begin the process.

(i) Spend a specified time (perhaps 15 minutes) individually with each of the parties, hearing 'their side of the story'. Focus the session on them and do not get hooked into agreeing with them or telling them what the other party said. Deflect questions such as 'don't you think that's unfair of her?', reminding them that you are an impartial party and are not there to find right or wrong in either of them.

(ii) Agree a time and place to bring the parties together and open the session by explaining that the aim is to find a way forward that both parties are happy with and that in order to achieve this, they will each have ten minutes uninterrupted time to share their point of view and then you will open it up for discussion. Agree some groundrules at this stage based around respect and not interrupting each other.

(iii) After hearing both parties' accounts, ask if either party wishes to respond to the other's account and allow them each time to do this. Then, clarify for both of them the key issues that have been discussed and any common ground you can see. Try to get the parties to look to the future to see how to improve the situation and not to focus on the past. Affirm both parties, build on any apology or concession, make sure that the parties 'hear' each other and keep the session balanced.

(iv) Now try and create a workable agreement (preferably written and signed by both parties) so that both parties can take away with them a clear way forward. Make sure the agreement is realistic and fair. Thank both parties for their valuable work and close the session.

(v) Evaluate the session with your co-mediator or by yourself. What worked well? What could be improved? How did you feel about the process?

NOTES:

It might be wise to use an outside mediator rather than yourself undertaking this role, as you have already built up relationships with the group members and may find it more difficult to be impartial. Even if you are impartial, they may perceive that you are not, and this will affect how they participate in the process. (*See* Resources for information on mediation services.)

4. Crisis Intervention

It may be that the situation has flared up to such an extent that a physical fight is imminent or is actually happening. Under these circumstances, your priority is obviously to break up the fight straight away and calm the situation down. It is advisable to get the other group members to leave the room or at least to move away if they are fuelling the situation, and to ask them to get help immediately from another worker if you are alone. Try to keep your voice grounded, firm and calm and your actions steady and centred. Once you have separated the disputants and another worker has arrived, sit down with one of them, whilst your co-worker or a colleague sits with the other, and give them both the opportunity to let off steam. Have an extended break if you need time to concentrate on the situation.

Try to find out what the fight was about, and decide what the most appropriate next step is (e.g. mediation).

CONFLICT SCENARIOS

Now you have some strategies to refer to, read through the following conflict scenarios and think through the issues you need to be aware of and any others you can think of. Which strategies, or any other ones you know, might be appropriate for which situations? Remember, the conflict might not be overt in the situation, but this does not mean that there is no need to address it.

> (a) A young woman starts to cry during a group exercise exploring families. Everyone stops working and a few of the participants put their arms around her and try to comfort her.

Issues to think about: How do you find an appropriate way of working with people's hurt and tears? What does this young woman need to be able to continue her work?

What do you do?

(b) One young man is not participating fully in exercises and is choosing not to take part in group discussions. You can sense that there is something wrong and that his self-exclusion is bothering other participants, but nobody says anything. You try and talk to him about it, one to one, but he says nothing is wrong. His behaviour does not change.

Issues to think about: How can you encourage the young man to participate or share what is concerning him? How can you prevent his increasing isolation from the rest of the group? How can you provide other group members space to share their unspoken frustrations?

What do you do?

(c) During a break, you suddenly hear screaming and shouting going on in the training room. You enter to find two young men on the project, Peter and Rob, face to face in an argument. Peter is in tears and Rob is taunting him, making the situation worse. Other group members come in to see what is happening.

Issues to think about: Is physical violence a possibility? What is needed immediately to calm down the situation? What is the effect of the other group members entering the room? Are you alone? Once you have calmed down the situation how do you move towards resolution?

What do you do?

(d) Sally comes to you after a session to tell you that she feels really threatened by one young man's behaviour and that she thinks he is abusing the trust in the group and using exercises to touch up the female group members. She doesn't want to speak to him but she wants it to stop.

Issues to think about: Is there a need to distinguish between Sally's feelings and whether this is actually happening? Should you encourage Sally to find a way of addressing the issue in a safe way with the group? If you speak to the young man, how should you approach the subject? Is there a need for some single-sex work?

What do you do?

(e) You have been working together for three weeks and have had problems with one young man whom other group members do not get along with and who they feel is sexist and racist. You have set up group discussions to address the young man's behaviour, as agreed in the contract, and spoken to him about it alone. You come back after a break to find that the group are refusing to continue working with this young man any more. He is alone in the training room and they are sitting together in the coffee bar.

Issues to think about: Has the young man acknowledged that his behaviour is upsetting other group members? Are the group breaking the groundrules themselves by refusing to work with him? Should he be left alone in the training room? Who is going to take responsibility for deciding on whether he is going to be asked to leave the group? What support does the young man need, if he is asked to leave?

What do you do?

(f) Two group members, Brian and Suzy, started going out with each other for a few weeks but have now split up because Suzy did not want to carry on. Brian is hurt and upset and starts to sulk in the sessions, as well as refusing to work with Suzy. He also starts to talk about her in the breaks to other group members. Suzy complains to you.

Issues to think about: How does Suzy view the situation? How can you support Brian to deal with his feelings in a way that doesn't impact negatively on the group? Is there more that needs to be said between them to resolve the situation?

What do you do?

THERE ARE NO RIGHT ANSWERS – BUT IT IS WORTH THINKING THROUGH HOW YOU MIGHT HANDLE SITUATIONS IF AND WHEN THEY ARISE.

MOVING ON FROM CONFLICT

After a situation of conflict has arisen and been addressed by the group, it is helpful to have some exercises prepared to move the group on. If the conflict was a serious one, emotions may be running high, and the group will be unsettled and in danger of losing its cohesion. Individually, they may need reassurance, and the group will need rebonding in order to return to the work in hand. Even if the conflict was a relatively mild one, you may still wish to undertake some work with the group, to re-establish the group's foundations, and offer some relaxation exercises.

1. Guided Meditation

Time:	20 minutes
Aim:	To guide the group through a short meditation.

DIRECTIONS:

Ask everyone to find a space on the floor and lie down, preferably on their backs with their arms by their sides and their knees raised. Explain that you are going to guide them through a journey in their mind, and that they need not share this with anyone else.

First they need to check their breathing. Ask them to take some deep breaths, and breathe in through the nose and out through the mouth, but not so much that they get dizzy, and just concentrate on this breathing for a few moments.

Now ask them to concentrate on the sounds they can hear in the room – the sound of your voice, other people breathing etc. Then ask them to concentrate on the sounds they can hear in the rest of the building; and finally, ask them to concentrate on the sounds they can hear outside the building.

Now ask them to imagine they are walking through a field on a beautiful summer's day. Ask them to imagine the details of the field, what flowers they can see, what colours and so forth. What can they hear? The aim is for them to be relaxed and calm, so encourage them to enjoy the sunny beauty of that place for a while.

Now start to bring them out of this meditative state, by gradually talking them back through the outside of the building sounds, the building sounds, and finally back to the sounds they can hear in the room, and the sound of their own breathing.

Tell them that they can move and sit up whenever they are ready – warn them to roll over onto their sides first, or else they may suffer dizziness.

FEEDBACK AND DISCUSSION:

You can bring the group together to feedback on this process, remembering that they do not need to share the details of their journey.

However, it may seem more appropriate to leave the participants in this relaxed state, and have a break before moving on.

NOTE:

There is no 'right' way of doing this exercise, as it is entirely for the benefit of the participants, and whatever they see or hear is appropriate for them.

2. Massage

Another way of relaxing the group and bringing them back together is through the physical sharing of a massage. This can be done in twos or as a whole group.

(a) Pairs Massage

There are several ways of doing this, and we have outlined three here:

Shake out: Each person takes it in turns to lie on the floor, whilst the other person raises different parts of their body from the floor, shakes them out, then gently lays them back down on the floor. The head should be done last, and very gently – the head is the heaviest part of the body, and it is very relaxing for another person to take the weight for a while. Be careful not to drop any part of the body back on the floor!

Journey on the back: Each person takes it in turns to stand behind the other one, and 'draw' a journey on their back, using their hands to create different rhythms of the weather, of different places. For example, if you were going through a jungle, you could trace your steps up the spine; then use broad strokes to indicate pushing through jungle creepers, then re-create a thunderstorm using different pressures and strokes, and so on.

Body massage: Each person takes it in turns to massage the other while they stand up, arms hanging loosely by their sides, legs slightly apart and knees slightly bent. Massage their arms and hands, their legs, their backs and their necks.

(b) Whole Group Massage

Again, there are several ways of doing this. One might be Rainstorm Massage (*see* Closings, Unit One) or simply form a line and give the person in front a body massage.

3. Gathering

A gathering can be a useful and non-threatening way of bringing the group back together. (*See* Group Work, Gatherings, Unit One.) Following a conflict situation, you should make sure that the gathering question is a positive one, that people will enjoy thinking about, for example, a place where you like to be and why.

4. Present Giving

Another way of re-creating a positive atmosphere is through giving the group 'presents'. Bring the group together in a circle and then ask everyone to think of something they would like to give to the group, such as the gift of laughter, or the gift of trust or the gift of creativity. Go round the group, asking everyone to put their hand into the middle, palm down, and say their gift. Finish with a group yell, with everyone throwing their hands in the air.

5. Enjoy Yourselves!

A conflict situation with the group can be a painful and challenging time. Group members will need space and time to express their feelings about what has happened, but they will also need the opportunity to engage with each other in a positive way again. As a facilitator, you can feed the group's mood by getting the group to play some games that they enjoy. This 'play' aspect of the work is equally important, and this is a good opportunity to remind the group to have some fun as well!

The exercises in this unit can be applied to the project at any given point, whether you are in the run-up phase, mid-leap, or even post-landing! They can offer the young people skills to transform their responses to conflict for ever, so don't be afraid to use them. The next unit completes your work with the group, providing you with suggestions for ending the project positively and responsibly for the young people.

UNIT SEVEN

THE NEXT STEP

Now we can look around at the new landscape we have arrived in, and decide what our choices are. This will help us to begin preparing to make the next leap.

Unit Seven: Ending

UNIT GUIDE:
Introduction
Guidance and Support
Recognising Achievements
Follow-Up

INTRODUCTION

It is always frightening as well as exciting to reach the end of something significant. There is the pride in having achieved something that you did not know you could, the feelings of relief for having some free time to yourself and the fear of not knowing what you are going to do next. You have made some friendships, but will they last? You have learnt a lot of new things but what difference will it make to your life now? Is it back to unemployment and depression or is it a step towards a brighter future? These are some of the thoughts and concerns that may be facing the young people at this final stage and it is vital that you encourage them and support them in identifying and making their next step.

GUIDANCE AND SUPPORT

The guidance and support you offer should be built into the whole of the project, rather than attached onto the end. It gives the participants the space to really focus on themselves, looking at their learning and emotional needs, as well as thinking realistically about their futures and creating new pathways and opportunities. Thinking about the future can start in Week One.

1. One-To-One

Allocating time each week to speak one-to-one with each participant is an invaluable way of hearing their concerns, asking them more challenging questions without the pressure of their peers, keeping a check on how they are coping, anticipating any problems before they arise, and helping them to systematically address their futures.

A useful framework for this type of meeting could be:

(a) *Check-In*: A brief chat on how they are doing generally.

(b) *Listen*: Hear their concerns, needs and feelings.

(c) *Feedback*: Offer them a chance to receive feedback on how you see their learning and development.

(d) *Goals and Obstacles*: Discuss their personal goals of what they would like to achieve during the project, for example to be more assertive in a group, and identify the obstacles that are preventing them. Look at how the obstacles can be overcome and the goal achieved.

(e) *Targets and Time Frame*: Help them to decide some targets for them to work towards and agree a time frame. Address what support they will need to achieve these targets. The targets can be very small, and must be realistic, so as not to set participants up to fail.

(f) *Reflection*: Go over what you have discussed and agreed and make sure it is helpful for them.

(g) *Check-Out*: A brief conversation to check on how that person is leaving the session.

As the sessions continue, you can check on their targets, negotiate new ones, affirm their progress, address new issues and introduce a section on 'beyond the end' to begin the process of planning what to do next.

VARIATIONS:

You might decide to set personal goals at the start of the project with the whole group, so that everyone can support each other in achieving their goals.

NOTES:

These one-to-one sessions are not counselling and you must be clear with your boundaries. You can refer participants to other services and it is advisable that you have this information available, but do not attempt to fulfil this role yourself. It will cloud your relationship with the young person and make it harder for them, especially when the project finishes and your responsibility ends.

2. Buddying

As well as you offering individual support to the participants, it is valuable for them to 'buddy' each other, providing mutual support and coaching. This idea

Figure 7.1 Thinking about the next step

may seem strange to the group at first, but they will find it very helpful in developing their own listening skills as well as offering additional support. Allocate 'buddy time' each week and offer some guidance on how to go about coaching each other through difficulties. You may decide to change buddies every fortnight, so that the group members do not form cliques, or you may prefer the continuity that the same buddies can provide.

3. Self-Support

It is vital that the young people learn how to support themselves to enable them to deal with life and create a positive future for themselves. They have, no doubt, already built up certain survival skills because they have had to, as a result of difficult life experiences. However, these may have an underlying theme of 'everyone else lets you down and you can't trust anybody' which is understandable but has certain costs for them as well as gains. You can encourage them to identify these costs and to learn how to ask for support when they need it. The drama work itself will result in participants becoming more self-aware and perhaps beginning to see patterns of behaviour that they wish to change.

Devising certain techniques, such as adopting a positive phrase which they can say to themselves when they are alone or feeling depressed, or making sure they treat themselves to something they enjoy, can help to build up their inner resources and develop their support skills. Use the one-to-one sessions to help them learn how to support themselves or dedicate a whole unit of work to 'how can I support myself?'

It will help the participants learn, if you know how to support yourself – so don't be afraid to ask for help if you need it too!

4. Referrals

Often accessing information is difficult for young people – not knowing where to look or not having the confidence to make contact with new organisations. You can help in a number of ways to ensure that the participants are moving on to something new and rewarding. Find a balance between making it easier for them and doing it for them – you provide the telephone number, but they do the calling.

- Collect information and flyers about other courses, other projects, voluntary work or employment opportunities, so that you become a resource for the young people to access.
- Create a comprehensive list of other opportunities that they could follow up with contact numbers.
- Discuss with them their individual interests (*see* One-To-One above).
- Rehearse with them what they need to say to prospective colleges or employers, if they feel unsure.

RECOGNISING ACHIEVEMENTS
Certificates

Receiving a piece of paper which recognises our learning and successes is very important for all of us, especially if we have never completed or passed anything in our lives before. For some of the young people on your project, this may be the first time they have ever received a certificate, and even though it may not be a qualification, it has a significance beyond its practical use. The certificate should be on special paper and contain basic information including the organisation's logo, the person's name, details of skills learned and experience gained on the project and the trainer(s)' signature(s).

Having a formal certificate-giving ceremony helps to mark the event and make it more memorable. You could call out each individual's name one by one and applaud them as they stand to receive their certificate and shake hands with you, or ask the Head of the organisation to hand them out.

Accreditation

Accrediting young people's learning is another way of recognising their achievements and may also be of substantial use to them if pursuing further education or employment opportunities. There are a number of different accrediting bodies which you could find out about. Try to select one which is flexible to your needs, affordable and meets the needs of the young people you work with. For example, the Open College Federation is a national accrediting body with regional divisions, and is ideal for accrediting practical courses and courses for disadvantaged groups. Equally, the Duke of Edinburgh Award scheme and the Youth Achievement Awards are ideal for young people. You might also want to find out about National Vocational Qualifications (NVQs). Remember to give yourself enough time to undertake this process – you will need to do this well in advance of running the project, or perhaps set it in motion for the next project.

FOLLOW-UP

The project has finished, but this does not mean that the young people's relationship with the organisation, or you, has to end abruptly – in fact it is important that this does not happen, especially after a full-time project. It is good practice to offer follow-up services to the young people you are working with and you may wish to identify with them what shape this will take. Here are a few suggestions, based on what we offer at Leap:

1. *Ongoing training sessions and support, for example a weekly workshop:* Ongoing training sessions are a safe, structured and supportive way to enable the young people to adjust to their life after the project. They provide:

- Contact with the workers and the organisation

- A meeting place for participants to socialise with each other and catch up on news

- A space for new skills to be learnt

- A space for learnt skills to be practised and confidence built

- A space to discuss needs and plans.

   Perhaps the sessions could involve a workshop element and a career guidance element. You could help individuals create their CVs or do practise job interviews. Set the agenda for the ongoing session with them to make sure it is fulfilling their needs.

2. *Newsletter*: A newsletter is a great way of keeping participants up to date with activities that the organisation is running now and in the future. Fill it with articles and photographs of the projects, written by the young people.

3. *Phone calls and contact*: Everyone appreciates a genuine interest being taken in their well-being and if you have half an hour available and access to a phone, why not give the participants a ring to see how they are doing? Showing this type of care and concern could be a lifeline for someone who is feeling isolated and alone.

4. *One-off workshops*: You could bring people together for a one-off, one-day workshop to refresh their skills, continue their training and also to double up as a reunion.

NOTE:

As well as follow-up being a responsible way of supporting the young people, it is also a useful way to monitor the success of your work (*see* Practicalities). How many young people have gone on to further education? How many have gained employment or voluntary work as a result of your training? This information is important to you and it provides useful evidence for funders as to the value of your work.

You have now completed the whole project, through from planning to evaluation and follow-up. In the following chapter are the practicalities you will need to think about when organising a project, whatever its size and scale.

PRACTICALITIES

CONTENTS

Introduction
Equal Opportunities Policy
Funding
The Budget
Booking a Tour
Health and Safety/ First Aid
Insurance
Space
Costume and Set
Tour Transport
Supervision
Documentation
Venue Evaluation
Tidying Up

INTRODUCTION

When undertaking any kind of project, it is important that organisational details are planned and addressed, in order to facilitate the smooth running of the project.

This section will help you consider these planning details, and give you tips on how to deal with them.

EQUAL OPPORTUNITIES POLICY

It is vital that your organisation has an equal opportunities policy, which it reviews regularly, and is committed to ensuring that the policy is active in practice as well as on paper. This policy should inform not only the recruitment and monitoring processes of staff and young people, but also your training practices, and it can be strengthened further by the group's own contract that they create for the sessions. Accessibility is the key to good equal opportunities practice. Brainstorm the barriers that can prevent young people from actively participating in a project – for example, no money, didn't hear about it, disabilities and so on. Then look at how to address these right from the start.

FUNDING

There are a range of resources to access for funding opportunities (*see* Resources), especially for a project such as this which can speak to a number of different funding criteria, including arts, education, youth and social welfare. You may find that raising money for an arts project is the least prosperous avenue to go down, and focusing on the issue you are addressing or the youth, education and training angle is the most resourceful. For example, Leap's 'Acting on Homelessness' project was funded primarily through its innovative work with young homeless people, rather than the theatre and drama outcomes. A good funding application will be well presented, providing specific aims and objectives with a clearly identified need, articulated outcomes and a realistic budget. Proven ability to undertake the work is always well received, so highlight any past work you or the organisation has successfully completed. Dissemination of outcomes, in the form of reports, publications, articles and videos, is also highly regarded and should be incorporated into the proposal if possible. If you can, try to build up a relationship with funders and follow up any expression of interest with an invitation to your site to see the work. Keep funders well informed as to the progress of the project and make sure that they are well acknowledged in all your publicity material.

THE BUDGET

Your project budget will obviously vary depending on your funding, numbers of staff, access to free resources etc. However, it is worth considering the following items when you break down your expenditure:

- Trainers' fees (including preparation and evaluation time)
- Production costs (costumes, set, props)
- Volunteers' travel expenses (Leap reimburses the trainees their travel expenses throughout the project)
- Transport costs (hire of van, fuel etc.)
- Publicity costs (for booking the tour)
- Postage and stationery (for mailout of publicity)
- Rent of rehearsal space
- Overheads (rent of office space, phone, heating, lights etc.)

- Administration costs
- Evaluation/documentation costs

BOOKING A TOUR

You will need access to certain administrative facilities in order to book the tour, including a phone, desktop publishing equipment, stationery and postage and someone in the office to carry out the necessary tasks whilst you are running the training. This person needs to be skilled in basic administration and producing publicity, and have up-to-date information about the show to respond accurately to enquiries. At Leap we offer this job to a volunteer who is familiar with the work and is interested in pursuing a career in arts administration.

Figure 8.1 Booking a tour

To book the tour you need:

- *Leaflets*: Leap tours to schools, youth clubs, homeless hostels, drop-ins and community centres to educate and entertain young people. We have ten years of experience, a good reputation, the issues we cover are relevant to young people's lives, the quality of the work is high, the initiative is peer-led and we are affordable for impoverished organisations. Make a list of *your* selling points. Decide on why venues will be interested in your work and make the most of it in your publicity leaflet. As well as focusing on your unique selling points, you will need to provide some basic information in the leaflet. What are the tour times and dates? What is the piece about? What is the length of the show and workshop? How many can participate in the workshop? What is the age range it targets? Are there any space requirements? How much does the performance and workshop cost? You will also benefit from providing some general information about your organisation, and any complimentary quotes from past venues. A tear-off slip is useful for those interested in a performance to return to you, asking for a contact name, address of venue, first and second choice of dates, and numbers and age of audience. At Leap we also request a deposit, of around 10 or 20 per cent. The leaflet is sent out with a covering letter to all the venues on our database.

- *A Database*: Where are you going to tour? Are you targeting every school and youth club in your area? How are you going to contact them? Do you have a database of all relevant organisations? If not, could you obtain a similar organisation's database, or ask another organisation to distribute your leaflet in their mailout? If you can, try to find the name of a contact person – it always helps to ensure that the leaflet will be read.

- *Follow-Up Phone Calls*: The value of making a follow-up phone call cannot be over-stressed. Teachers and youth workers have busy schedules, and, despite their intention to book the show, they may well not do it unless prompted by a phone call from you. Make sure you phone at a time when you are likely to catch the teacher in the staff room – either early morning, lunchtime or after school; similarly youth workers are mostly available in the afternoons and early evenings.

- *A Tour Schedule*: At Leap, we tour Monday to Thursday, totalling seven shows a week. Touring is tiring and you want to avoid the combination of early mornings and late nights wherever possible. Work out a tour schedule which reduces the amount of driving, bearing in mind where different venues are located and trying to schedule ones in the same area on the same day. Create a tour schedule, detailing each day of the tour with the venue's name, address, time of performance and audience make-up, and give it to the participants.

- *Confirmation of Booking*: It is worth writing to each venue to confirm time, place and date of booking. This is to minimalise any mistakes by identifying them at an early stage.

- *Publicity Material*: Some venues (e.g. schools) may have an established audience and not need to publicise the performance. However, if the venue wishes to attract public interest in the performance they have booked, they will find a poster and flyers very useful. It is worth having posters available for venues, with space to fill in the time, date and cost details as is appropriate to them.

HEALTH AND SAFETY/FIRST AID

The space you work in needs to be appropriate and conform to health and safety regulations, and you will need to inform participants of fire exits and the organisation's fire drill. If you have any concerns, ask a senior worker in the organisation. Make sure that there is a first aid officer on site. Perhaps you could undertake a course in first aid?

It is also worth having a registration form for participants to complete on induction, requesting any medical details they feel you should know about (including recent injuries, allergies and medical conditions) plus a person to contact in case of an emergency.

INSURANCE

Make sure you have public liability insurance to cover you for all your work with volunteers and trainees, including the tour. It is also worth insuring any special equipment, for example, musical instruments.

SPACE

It is very important that you and the group have a space that you can work in properly. This means that it should be used only by this group for the specified time so they can concentrate and focus on the work in hand, and not be interrupted by people going in and out, or other activities, or telephones ringing. The group need to feel ownership of the space for this time, so that they can express themselves in the drama or in discussions without being interrupted or laughed at, and so, if they want, they can put things on the wall and leave them there, without them getting defaced or damaged.

It is also ideal to have a separate informal space for breaks and lunch etc. to keep the social time and work time clearly defined.

COSTUME AND SET

As mentioned in Unit Three, costumes for the show need only consist of a basic outfit that all the group members wear, such as black jogging pants and a red T-shirt for example, and which signifies a neutral state. Added to this, there will be items of clothing that can signify a character, such as a hat or scarf, that can be taken on and off quickly.

If you decide you need more elaborate costumes, or you need something specific, such as a historical outfit, you can hire costumes but this could prove expensive. Alternatively, you could contact a local drama school or amateur theatre company and ask if they have anything suitable that you could borrow, or you could try local professional theatre companies or theatres, as they may have a wardrobe section that you could borrow from or perhaps hire at a low cost.

Again, the set need only be simple, consisting of a backdrop that can be folded up and carried away, and maybe some chairs in each venue. Try contacting your local art college to see if they have a theatre design section, and to see if one of the students might be interested in doing this for you to gain experience. If the backdrop design is a multi-purpose one, then you can use it again for other shows.

TOUR TRANSPORT

If your organisation does not own a van, you will need to hire one for the duration of the tour. Local authorities normally have a selection of minibuses that can be hired by community organisations, although you may have to become a member. This means that you will need to budget for the hire of the van, and book it well in advance of when you need it. As the driver, you may need to take the local authority test to qualify you to drive it, so again allow time for this.

SUPERVISION

Good supervision and support is as important for you running the project as it is for the people taking part. The organisation you are working for should offer line management, which ensures that accountability is clear and formalised. If it doesn't, you may wish to raise this as a concern and ask for the issue to be clarified. Also, you may decide to make a request for non-managerial support to provide you with a much needed space to discuss training concerns, focus on your own learning needs and share concerns and difficulties that you may be having. Do not underestimate the drain that a full-time project will have on you and the benefits that can be gained from accessing effective support and supervision.

DOCUMENTATION (see also Evaluation, Unit Five)

The show can be documented in several ways:

1. *Script*: Once the show is up and running, you can ask people to write up the lines of the scenes they have worked on, and then type this up so that you have a record of the script.

2. *Video*: You could also video a performance of the show, perhaps at the public performance, giving you another record of the work. The local youth service may have a camera you can hire out or borrow, or you could ask if any of the participants know someone with a camera who would be willing to do it, perhaps a film student who may be able to edit it for you as well. You may need to pay a small sum for this, so remember to budget for it.

   Be aware that live performance can be difficult to capture on video, and that it may not quite encapsulate the atmosphere of the show. However, it can be useful to have it to show future funders, and it is also fun for the participants to watch themselves.

3. *Photographs*: It is great to have a good set of photographs to record the show and workshop. Not only does this allow participants to order their own copies, but it also means that you can create laminated panels to exhibit your work where suitable.

4. *Facilitator's Report*: At the end of the project, it is very useful for the facilitator(s) to write a report of the whole experience. This offers you the chance to evaluate the work overall and to make recommendations for future projects, which will be useful for both you and any future workers, as well as being available to show

funders and other interested organisations. The writing of the report should be budgeted for as an integral part of the project.

Report Structure:

At Leap, we structure the report to include information which will be of interest to the management committee, future project directors and funders. This makes it quite substantive, and you may wish to be briefer in your approach. There may also be other things you want to add that are particularly relevant to your organisation or are stipulated in funding agreements. We include a list of recommendations under every section, as well as overall recommendations at the end of the report.

1. TITLE PAGE AND CONTENTS

2. NAMES OF PARTICIPANTS

3. BACKGROUND INFORMATION

   - The organisation and previous work
   - The dates, aims and objectives of the project
   - Brief outline of the project

4. MONITORING AND RECRUITMENT

   - Recruitment of facilitators
   - Recruitment of participants, including where the project was advertised, what the response was, how many people attended introductory workshops, breakdown of participants by race, gender, etc.
   - Recommendations

5. FACILITATORS' PREPARATION AND RESEARCH

6. BREAKDOWN OF THE TRAINING PROGRAMME

7. THE PROJECT

   - Description of the training and devising period: how it was planned and carried out, any problems or outstanding events, how the group worked together etc.
   - Recommendations

8. THE TOUR

   - Breakdown of venues, including contact name and number

- Short description of each show
- Description of the tour: a summary of how it was received, any problems or events, how the group coped etc.
- Recommendations

9. THE SPEAK OUT (where relevant)

- Description of the Speak Out: where, when, who spoke, how it went, any follow-up etc.
- Recommendations

10. EVALUATIONS

- Breakdown of evaluations by host venues, including quotes of appropriate comments
- Hopes and fears comments by participants (anonymous)
- Quotes from participants' evaluation forms (anonymous)
- Facilitators' personal evaluations – an honest reflection of the project, including thanks, suggestions and ideas

11. FINAL RECOMMENDATIONS

- Overall recommendations for future projects

12. APPENDICES

- Included in this could be photos, letters, the Speak Out programme, any poems or song lyrics written by participants, resources or contact addresses not included elsewhere.

VENUE EVALUATION

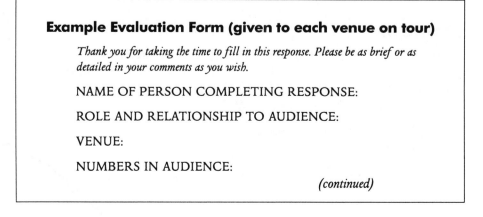

Example Evaluation Form (given to each venue on tour)

Thank you for taking the time to fill in this response. Please be as brief or as detailed in your comments as you wish.

NAME OF PERSON COMPLETING RESPONSE:

ROLE AND RELATIONSHIP TO AUDIENCE:

VENUE:

NUMBERS IN AUDIENCE:

(continued)

Example Evaluation Form (continued)

PLEASE CAN YOU GIVE A ROUGH BREAKDOWN OF THE
AUDIENCE BY ETHNICITY, AGE AND GENDER:

*Please respond by using the points system illustrated below. Any additional
comments are very much appreciated.*

1 = Excellent   2 = Very Good   3 = Good   4 = Fair   5 = Poor

PRE-SHOW COMMUNICATION

THE EVENT

1. How would you rate the performance part of the event? Any
comments?

2. How would you rate the workshop part of the event? Any
comments?

3. What did you feel about the relationship of the company with
the audience/participants during the workshop?

4. How suitable was the event for the age range of your group?

5. Was the company's presentation useful to the longer-term aims of
your work? If so, in what ways?

6. What do you think your group gained most from Leap's visit?

THE FUTURE

1. What issues would you and your group like to see explored in a
future Leap presentation?

2. Any further comments that you would like to make about the
whole event or the Leap project in general?

TIDYING UP

There is always a certain amount of clearing up to do after a project and also a
certain amount of resistance to doing it! Make sure the organisation you are
working for recognises this need and schedules paid time to carry it out.

A few ideas for tidying-up areas follow:

- Cleaning and putting away costumes
- Putting away and returning props

- Filing research information on the issue
- Cleaning and returning the van
- Going through flipchart papers and discarding or transcribing them.

EPILOGUE

SUMMING UP

Congratulations on *making a leap*! Whether you have run your first workshop, planned a series of sessions, or completed a full-time project, you deserve to be acknowledged for your achievement and to be recognised for the hard work, commitment, energy and patience that has no doubt been required of you.

We hope that you have found this manual a useful guide and reference point for your work, and that you can continue to refer to it, or recommend it to others, who are embarking on creative drama work with young people.

Perhaps you can reflect on *the leap* that you, yourself, have made over the course of your drama work. What new choices do you have? What 'different place' are you at now, than when you first began? What is your next step?

Good luck.

RESOURCES

Books: References and Further Reading

Acland, A. (1990) *A Sudden Outbreak of Common Sense: Managing Conflict Through Mediation*. London: Hutchinson Business Books.

Barker, C. (1977) *Theatre Games: A New Approach to Drama Training*. London: Eyre Methuen Publishers.

Berry, C. (1973) *Voice and the Actor*. London: Hatton Publishers.

Boal, A. (1992) *Games for Actors and Non-Actors*. London: Routledge.

Brandes, D. and Phillips, H. (1979) *Gamesters' Handbook*. London: Hutchinson Education.

Brown, P. and Smyth, J. (1997/98) *A Guide to Company Giving*. London: Directory of Social Change.

Brown, P. and Smyth, J. (1997/98) *A Guide to the Major Trusts* (Vol.2). London: Directory of Social Change.

Brown, P. and Smyth, J. (1998) *A Guide to UK Company Giving*. London: Directory of Social Change.

Eastwood, N. (1997) *The Youth Funding Guide*. London: Directory of Social Change in association with NYA.

Fine, N. and Macbeth, F. (1992) *Fireworks: Creative Approaches to Conflict.* Leicester: Youth Work Press.

Fine, N. and Macbeth, F. (1992) *Playing with Fire.* Leicester: Youth Work Press.

Forrester, S. (1997/98) *The Arts Funding Guide.* London: Directory of Social Change.

Holly, K. (1996) *The Guide to Local Trusts.* London: Directory of Social Change.

Huskins, J. (1996) *Quality Work with Young People.* London: Youth Clubs UK.

Jackson, T. (1993) *Learning Through Theatre.* London: Routledge.

Jennings, S. (1986) *Creative Drama in Groupwork.* Bicester: Winslow Press.

Johnston, K. (1981) *Impro: Improvisation and the Theatre.* London: Eyre Methuen Publishers.

Liebmann, M. (ed.) (1996) *Arts Approaches to Conflict.* London: Jessica Kingsley Publishers.

Neelands, J. (1990) *Structuring Drama Work: A Handbook of Available Forms in Theatre and Drama.* Cambridge: Cambridge University Press.

Oddey, A. (1995) *Devising Theatre.* London: Routledge.

O'Toole, J. and Haseman, B. (1986) *Dramawise: An Introduction to GCSE Drama.* London: Heinemann Educational Books.

Schutzman, M. and Cohen-Cruz, J. (ed.) (1994) *Playing Boal.* London: Routledge.

Williamson, H. (ed.) (1995) *Social Action for Young People.* Dorset: Russell House Publishing Ltd.

Organisations

AVP London (Alternatives to Violence Project)
BM AVP
London WC1N 3XX
Tel: 0171 820 9170

The Alternatives to Violence Project was developed in New York state prisons to allow inmates to look at their behaviour and explore new ways of resolving conflict. In Britain, AVP volunteers run workshops in the community and in prisons to enable all kinds of people to do the same thing.

Centrepoint (Head Office)
2 Swallow Place
London W1
Tel: 0171 544 5000

Centrepoint is a national charity for young homeless people, providing emergency shelter, short-term and longer term accomodation, peer education projects and training opportunities as well as campaigning to prevent youth homelessness and raise awareness of the issues.

Cities in Schools (Tower Hamlets)
91 Brick Lane
London E1 6QN
Tel: 0171 247 9489

Cities in Schools is an educational charity which aims to maximise young people's potential and ensure their rightful integration into the community.

Leap Confronting Conflict
8 Lennox Road
Finsbury Park
London N4 3NW
Tel: 0171 272 5630

Leap Confronting Conflict is a voluntary youth service organisation working with young people and those who work with them to confront conflict creatively in their lives. Leap runs training courses for professionals, projects for young people and volunteers, and publishes training materials on conflict resolution (see resources 'Fireworks' and 'Playing with Fire'). Leap Theatre Workshop can be contacted at the same address.

Mediation UK
Alexander House
Telephone Avenue
Bristol BS1 4BS
Tel: 0117 904 6661

Mediation UK is the umbrella organisation for all the mediation and reparation schemes in the UK.

National Drama
c/o London Drama
Central School of Speech and Drama
Eton Avenue
London NW3 3HY
Tel: 0171 722 4730

National Drama is the largest professional organisation for drama educators in the UK. The association is pro-active in the fields of in-service education, curriculum development, research, publications and in the lobbying of government and other arts bodies to promote the cause of drama in education.

Augusto Boal
Theatre of the Oppressed
Rua Francisco Otaviano 185/41
CEP 22080, Ipanema, Arpoador
Rio de Janeiro, RJ
Brazil

Augusto Boal is a Brazilian theatre director, writer and theorist. His work is renowned throughout the world for its use of theatre as a tool for personal and social change. He has theatre centres in Rio and in Paris.

The City Kids Foundation
57 Leonard Street
New York
NY 10013
Tel.+1 (212) 925 3320

The City Kids Foundation develops the leadership potential of youth by engaging them in an educational and artistic process that is grounded in the grass-roots philosophy of safe space, peer education and multicultural bridge building.

LIST OF GAMES
AND EXERCISES

Unit One: Preparation

Three Name Games	40
Three Fact Games	41
Person to Person	43
Points of Contact	43
Touch Three Things	45
Bums on Seats	45
Tag Games	46
Bomb and Shield	47
Greet, Argue and Make Up	47
Dangerous Places	48
Wink Murder	49
Lawyer	49
Are You Ready?	50
Zip Zap Boing	51
Jailbreak	52
Three Blind Mice	53
Hands Off	54
Trust Circles	55
Three Ways to Fall	56
Cat and Mouse II	57
Grandmother's Keys	58
Frogs and Alligators	59
Giants, Wizards, Elves	60
Saints and Sinners	60
Who Started the Movement?	61
The Contract	62
Brainstorming	66
Gatherings	67
Hopes and Fears	68
Paper not Floor	68
Daily and Weekly Feedback	69
Three Ways of Listening	70
What's on Top of Your Pile?	71
Mirrors	71
Personal Road Maps	72
Personal Storytelling	72
Where Do You Stand?	73
Tropical Rainstorm	74
Rainstorm Massage	75
Pass the Pulse	76
Get Knotted	76

Count One to Twenty	77
Circle Sitting	77
Texan Yell	77
Make 'em Laugh	77
Affirmation Pyramid	78
Go-Rounds	78

Unit Two: Training

The Tree	84
Physical Warm-Up	85
Vocal Warm-Up	88
States of Tension	93
Status	95
Community Build Role Play	97
Improvisation Games:	99
Mime a Lie	99
Change the Action	100
In the Manner of the Word	100
Change the Object	100
Persuasion	101
Magic Box	101
Pick Up	102
Impro-Tag	102
Argument Down the Line	103
Storytelling:	104
One Word Story	104
Whose Story is it Anyway?	105
A Modern Day Fairy Tale	106
Image Storytelling	106
Bard's Chair	106
Voice and Sound:	107
Call and Echo	107
Circle Music	108
The Band	109
Sound Pictures	110
Machines	111
Physical Theatre:	112
Isolating Movement/Body Awareness	112
Stylising Action/Movement into Theatre	113
Physicalising Objects	114
Physicalising Places	114

Essential Movement 115
Physicalising Stories 116
Image Work: 116
  Mill, Grab and Tab 117
  What's the Story? 117
  Circle Turn 118
  Group Images 119
The Forum Technique 122
Working with Young People 126
Workshop Styles 127
Roles in a Hat 127
Running Small Sections 128
Co-Leading 129

Unit Three: Devising the Show
Aims of Educational Theatre 134
Aims of this Particular Piece 135
The Triangle 136
The Character Outline 141
Developing the Character: 143
  Character History 143
  Hotseating 143
  Building a Picture 143
  A Day in the Life of 145
  Animal Characters 145
Making Scene One 148
Making Scenes Two and Three 149
The Ingredients of a Scene 149
Non Character Scenes: 151
  Facts into Theatre 152
  Exploring Stereotypes 154
  Commenting on the Issue
    as a Whole Group 157
  Case Studies 158
The Facilitator as Director 162
Rehearsal Preparation 164
Rehearsal Strategies: 165
  Line Run 166
  Speed Run 166
  Singing Run 167
  What Are You Thinking? 167
Devising the Workshop 171
Hotseating 172
Leadership Skills 173

Unit Four: The Tour
Where's Maria? 180
Ball of Energy 181

Unit Five: Evaluation
Purposes of Evaluation 198
Evaluation Methods: 199
  Individual 199
  Pairs 199
  Small Groups: 200
  Whole Group Work 202

Unit Six - Confronting Conflict
Individual Alphabetical Brainstorm 210
Four Word Build 211
Changing the Pattern 213
'I' Statements 214
Listening Exercise 216
Drama is Conflict: 217
  Look at it Both Ways! 217
  Changing the Outcome 219
  Mirror Mirror 220
Mediation 220
Conflict Scenarios 222
Guided Meditation 225
Massage 226
Gathering 227
Present Giving 227
Enjoy Yourselves! 227